The ARA Messages

A collection of dreams, visions, and spiritual communications by

HAROLD SHERMAN

Compiled and Edited by
Saskia Praamsma

SQUARE CIRCLES PUBLISHING

THE ARA MESSAGES
A collection of dreams, visions,
and spiritual communications
by Harold Sherman

Compiled and Edited by Saskia Praamsma

Copyright © 2012 Saskia Praamsma
All Rights Reserved

Corrected November 2016

Cover design: Syrp & Co.

Cover art: *Awakening* by Bessie Lasky
from the collection of Saskia Praamsma

The original documents are located among
Harold Sherman's papers in the Special Collections
at the Torreyson Library, University of Central Arkansas
at Conway; Jimmy Bryant, Director.

ISBN: 978-0-9967165-2-9

Square Circles Publishing
www.squarecirclespublishing.com

Contents

	Introduction	v
1	Dreams and Impressions	1
2	First Ara Messages 1938-1941	19
3	Hollywood—May 1941	27
4	Hollywood—September 1941	48
5	Hollywood—October 1941	73
6	Hollywood—November 1941	84
7	Hollywood—January 1942	107
8	Further Communications	129
9	Poems	151

Introduction

HAROLD SHERMAN (1898-1987) was a lifelong student of parapsychology and the mysteries of the mind. His long list of self-help books, starting with *Your Key to Happiness* in 1935, were read by millions. He was also a popular lecturer, traveling across the United States to spread the message that man needs to know how to utilize the power of his own mind before he can be happy and live life to the fullest.

Sherman's wife Martha, whom he first met in kindergarten in Traverse City, Michigan, and with whom he spent his entire adult life, shared in these studies. Most of his books were first dictated to her, and together they would discuss and revise them before publication.

A major influence on both of their lives was a mysterious figure named Harry J. Loose. Martha Sherman, in 1992, recalled the story of their meeting:

> In the summer of 1921, married less than a year, we were living in Marion, Indiana, where Harold was employed as a reporter for the *Marion Chronicle*—his first writing job.
>
> This July afternoon he had been assigned to cover a lecture being given by a Harry J. Loose for the Redpath-Chautauqua circuit, which in those years was a popular means of bringing outside thinking to small communities in the Midwest. Harold had taken me with him and we had found Mr. Loose's lecture on "Crime and Criminology," as it then existed in the big city of Chicago, fascinating. As we discussed it on our way home, Harold

felt he would be able to cover it in an interesting way for the paper.

However, Harold then remarked that he felt impelled to see Mr. Loose again that evening, although he couldn't see why as he already had all the information he needed for the article. Since I had early learned to honor the odd decisions Harold made from time to time, I raised no objection, and after our simple evening meal he left again for the downtown area.

He slowly wandered around the town square, wondering why he had followed this silly notion, but finally stepped into the lobby of the unimposing Marion Hotel and inquired of the clerk behind the desk, whom he did not know, "Would Harry Loose be registered at this hotel?"

Without asking Harold's name, the clerk turned around, buzzed a number, and announced: "A gentleman in the lobby to see you, sir." Harold could hear a strong voice on the other end reply, "Send him up, please."

"Second floor, Room 22, across from the elevator," directed the clerk.

Still wondering, Harold took the old-time, clanking elevator and, as he stepped out on the second floor, knocked hesitantly at the partially open door.

"Come in, Sherman!" came the answer; and as Harold entered the room, "You're late. I have been expecting you for half an hour."

On the bed, propped up with pillows, sat Harry Loose in his BVDs! It was a hot night, long before air-conditioning. This informal attitude and greeting completely knocked any previously conceived approach out of Harold's mind. "I don't really know why I'm here," he stumbled, "but I did find your afternoon lecture very interesting."

Then followed the most interesting evening of Harold's life, as Mr. Loose proceeded to tell him the real reason for his lecture tour. He related that a ninety-six-year-old woman in Boston had required him to contact young people of potential higher mental and spiritual development on the circuit and to make them aware of the possibility of some unknown service in the years ahead. He then began to demonstrate unusual faculties, such as, "See that handkerchief on the dresser? I do not have to get off the bed to get it." And, as Harold watched, the handkerchief was suddenly in Mr. Loose's hands.[1]

Mr. Loose proceeded to show an intimate knowledge of the details of Harold's life and some of the potentials, ending up with a demonstration of telepathy between himself and his wife, then in Chicago, adding that it would be several years—ten or more—before his and Harold's paths would cross again....

About two weeks later, Harold received a handwritten letter in which Mr. Loose again indicated his intimate knowledge of Harold, his personality and habits. We treasured this letter carefully.

The years passed with no further word from or about Harry Loose. Harold had, from time to time, tried to make contact with him but he seemed to have vanished. He had not lectured for Redpath for years and no one knew what had become of him.

In the meantime, we had moved to New York City where Harold, after many ups and downs, had become a modestly successful author of boys' sport, adventure and humorous stories and books. But the fascination with the potentials of the human mind never left him, and he pursued its study as well as evidences of the supernormal whenever possible.

Finally, in 1937, the opportunity to conduct serious exploration came as Harold sat talking with Sir Hubert

---

[1] This incident does not appear in Harold's own published accounts of his first meeting with Loose.

Wilkins at the City Club of New York. Sir Hubert was about to start on a serious rescue mission for the Russian government. Three Russian planes had attempted to fly non-stop over the North Pole to the United States—a daring adventure in those times. Two had made it successfully, landing on the West Coast, but the third had been lost over the polar ice and Sir Hubert, an experienced pilot, had been asked to see if he could locate it. As the two men talked, it occurred to them that telepathy could be helpful if lost on the ice. Because of the intense interest in beginning air travel, as well as the difficulties of communication in those days, these experiments brought national attention and were headlined in the daily news.[2] Letters began to pour in, among them one from Walter M. Germain, chief of police in Saginaw, Michigan. As Harold held the letter in his hand, something seemed to say, "This man knows the whereabouts of Harry J. Loose." Responding to the impulse, Harold wrote Mr. Germain and had an immediate response: 123 Elizabeth Street, Monterey Park, California! . . .

Harold wrote to that address, Harry Loose replied, and a correspondence resumed between the two men.

Through their "flow of astounding letters," as Harold later described them, Harry Loose became the Shermans' spiritual mentor. He told them about a book of divinely revealed information—the Book of Urantia—that was being prepared for publication, which Loose believed would change the thinking of the world. He said that he himself had somehow been involved in the development of the manuscript, which was in the custody of a well-known psychiatrist, Dr. William Sadler, at his residence at 533 Diversey Parkway in Chicago. The manuscript was studied

---

[2] These experiments were described in the March 1939 issue of *Cosmopolitan* magazine and in *Thoughts Through Space* (New York: Creative Age Press, 1942), co-authored by Sherman and Wilkins.

and discussed by members of a small group called the Forum, who had signed an oath not to discuss it with outsiders.[3]

Six years before reconnecting with Loose, Harold had been granted exclusive rights, by the Mark Twain Estate, to dramatize the life of the famed author and had written a play, *Mark Twain*. While it was being considered by Broadway producers, veteran Hollywood producer Jesse L. Lasky secured the film rights and hired Harold to collaborate on the screen treatment. In May 1941, while Martha and their daughters (Mary aged 20 and Marcia 12) stayed behind in New York, Harold was brought to Hollywood by Warner Bros. for a few weeks' preliminary work, which gave him the chance to talk with Loose face to face.

Intrigued by what Loose said about the Urantia project, Harold and Martha became interested in joining the Forum. After a brief trip back East to finalize his contract and to collect Martha and the girls, the Shermans went to Chicago and applied for membership. Martha explains the circumstances:

> While living in Indiana in the early 1920s, we had studied psychic phenomena with our friends, Dr. Merrill and Josephine ("Jo") Davis. . . . We recalled that at one time she had mentioned that she had an uncle [*sic*—cousin] in Chicago—a doctor and psychiatrist—who was also interested in the subject, but at that time we had not pursued his identity. However, these many years later, we recalled her reference and found that, indeed, his name was Dr. William Sadler! We asked her to write him a letter of introduction for us, which she was happy to do. This opened the way for a brief stop in Chicago as we drove west.

After meeting Dr. Sadler and the group, and officially joining the Forum, the family traveled to California, reaching Hol-

---

[3] If Loose had signed this oath, he clearly broke it.

lywood in mid-August. Frequent visits between the Shermans and Loose and his wife, Emily, followed.

The Shermans remained in Hollywood until May 1942, when they moved to Chicago to study the Urantia papers. For five years they lived across the street from 533 Diversey Parkway, during which time they kept a detailed diary consisting of sixteen handwritten notebooks of their experiences.[4]

•••

In transcribing the diaries and letters, starting in 2000, I encountered mysterious references to a "little black book" containing psychic impressions and "Ara messages":

> Gradually, you are touching upon elements in me which have risen to the surface of consciousness from deep down within, giving me visions and impressions which I have copied in my "little black book."
> —*Harold to Harry Loose, March 12, 1941*

> Today came your second letter written en route[5] with the additional inspirational suggestions. . . . I shall place them in our little black book.
> —*Martha to Harold, May 17, 1941*

> We devoted the entire a.m., Harold having developed an idea for a new book under the title *The Great Adventure of Your Soul*, to rereading the messages received from Ara while in California. . . .
> —*Diary, October 1, 1942*

---

[4] *The Sherman Diaries* are published by Square Circles Publishing in five volumes: *Volume One: Dawning Revelations 1898-1942* (2002); *Volume Two: Revelation and Rebellion 1942* (2003); *Volume Three: Aftermath of Rebellion 1943*; (2004); *Volume Four: The Turning Point 1944-1945* (2005); *Volume Five: Moving On 1946-1955* (2008).

[5] Harold was on his way to Hollywood to work on the *Mark Twain* treatment.

No such messages were to be found among the Harold Sherman papers at the University of Central Arkansas in Conway. Knowing that the Shermans would not have disposed of this material, I asked their daughter, Marcia, at that time living in her parents' Arkansas home, which still contained many of their books and papers, to try to locate the "little black book." Marcia had not heard of it before, but not long after she phoned me, saying, "I found it!"

It was a small, black three-ring binder containing Harold's visions, dream impressions, and other inspirational messages typed up and neatly assembled in chronological order. Mostly it contained messages from "Ara," Harold's name for what Loose called the Comforter or Thought Adjuster, the voice of God within.

Not all the dreams referred to were found inside the black binder. Over the next few years Marcia would report from time to time the discovery of yet another "lost" message or dream impression, slipped between the pages of a book or mixed in with a different stack of papers.

During one of my visits to the Sherman home, Marcia graciously allowed me to copy all the newfound material before she donated the documents to the Harold Sherman collection at UCA. The various impressions and the contents of the "little black book" are presented in this volume.

•••

The dreams and impressions started to come to Harold in 1937, around the time of his ESP experiments with Sir Hubert Wilkins which resulted in their jointly written book, *Thoughts Through Space* (1942).

In May 1941, still in New York and inspired by Loose's teachings, Harold began receiving his Ara inspirations, and after reconnecting with Loose again during his short trip to California later that month, the messages increased. When later that year the family moved to Hollywood, Harold received the major portion of the Ara messages, obviously inspired by the teachings Loose was imparting. After the Shermans' move to Chicago in May 1942, the messages and poems became heavily influenced by the Urantia teachings as well as by the events of World War II.

•••

I wish to express my gratitude to Marcia Sherman Lynch and Mary Sherman Kobiella, the daughters of Harold and Martha Sherman, who have unfailingly cooperated with me in my efforts to preserve their parents' legacy, and who, in the process, have become treasured friends.

>   Saskia Praamsma
>   Bilthoven, the Netherlands
>   November 2016

The Messages

1

Dreams and Impressions

1938-1941

New York
January 1938

Since I have been carrying on these telepathic experiments with Wilkins, I seem to have awakened channels in consciousness which have brought me unusual dreams of different civilizations or planes. Here is one of the most vivid of these experiences.

I found myself, with Martha, attired in a form of luxurious evening dress. I do not recall just what I was wearing, except the feeling that I was well-appointed, but Martha was radiantly beautiful in a rich, purple gown which trailed as she walked. A bejeweled star shone at her throat, and this, with her dark eyes and hair made a stunning picture.

We were apparently paying a visit to some important personages and were just arriving at their residence. But the buildings of this very advanced civilization were much different from those of today. They were built in great circular, tubular tiers, like mammoth automobile tires piled one upon another with a common entrance on one side—the tires being joined and compacted at this side but separating at various angles on the opposite sides so that each circular tier of dwelling places stood out into space alone and distinct.

This building was of tremendous height. Entering at a point or level midway between the top and bottom by our modernized car or conveyance, which I remember only indistinctly, carrying us right inside, we got out and the car was immediately discharged, apparently by some magnetic force, to its parking place.

I was conscious of a myriad of great passageways, some sloping up and circling around and around onto the different circular tubing levels. Martha and I passed through a great reception room, high-ceilinged, something like the Radio City Music Hall, but much grander in size and architecture. We crossed this apparent lobby, passing many impressive men and women, all handsomely dressed and all apparently knowing exactly where they were going.

We stepped into some kind of an elevator and I felt ourselves being transported upward, easily and silently, a great distance. We got out upon a certain tier. I recall now simply having spoken the number of this tier while in the elevator and this had started the mechanism.

Walking out along the corridor at this level was somewhat like being in the salon of a Zeppelin for we could see for miles, as we followed around the circular tube, every time we came to a great, circular window. In one direction, I remember a great expanse of ocean in the distance. In another, hundreds of other great dwellings like the one we were in.

The scene now appeared to be night, with all the circular, porthole-like windows gleaming or glowing with an inner light, making the whole outer world look like dazzling bands of luminosity as far as the eye could see.

I had the impression that everything one could wish for in this life was contained in each one of these great buildings, and yet Martha and I accepted what we saw, for the most part, as though we were accustomed to it.

Only once did I feel wonderment and make an inquiry and that was when we came into a great music room and Martha went over to a mammoth organ unlike anything I have ever seen, seated herself, and commenced playing music of indescribable beauty. (Martha plays no musical instrument in this life.)

I listened, spellbound, overwhelmed in admiration. It seemed that the beauty of her soul was being transmuted to music—or that I was hearing, for the first time, the *music of her soul!*

I suddenly felt a presence and turned to find a kindly-appearing, mature-aged gentleman regarding me, smilingly.

"To whom are we indebted for this?" I heard myself ask him. And he, giving me an unforgettable knowing look, said quietly, "You may refer to me as the *Governor.*"

When Martha had finished at the organ, which was played by pushing a myriad of buttons rather than keys, she dismounted from the sumptuous seat and took my arm, and we continued on toward our destination on this same circular level.

I was conscious that magnificent dwellings were enclosed in these great circular tiers opening off these corridors. We stopped at a certain door and spoke, I believe, the name "Byron," when the door opened by unseen hand, and we stepped inside to be greeted by a charming man and wife who stood side by side as they took our hands in greeting.

The scene dissolved as though we were not supposed to remember what transpired there.

The next thing of which I was conscious was awakening to find myself on the outer side of a huge bed, with Martha, at an elevation above a corridor, or overlooking a passageway. I had been awakened by the voices of a couple passing below who were unconscious of our presence even though they were extremely near us.

The impression was most vivid and I seemed to understand what they were saying as I lay there and watched them going by. But something at this moment *actually* awakened me and as I came to my *outer* consciousness, in my own bed, I carried over the impression of my dream momentarily into this dimension, for the couple now *stood*, for a second, *beside my bed talking.*

I looked up and saw them, conscious they were talking a language now foreign to my ears. I had no sense of fear—only of great interest—and, as I became wider awake, they faded from external sight and hearing, even as I looked.

My lasting impression, with this dream (?) over, was one of great inner happiness, as though Martha and I had been on some mission in space together, and were developed with powers beyond our conscious awareness, being much more closely united than we have any imagining.

New York
February 3, 1938

This morning, after my wife had arisen to see our younger daughter, Marcia, off to school, I rolled over for a last little nap and had the following dream:

I seemed to have stepped into the City Club and found a heavy envelope, especially bound, from Wilkins, postmarked "February 6th," containing copies of my impressions covering more than two months, with his usual marginal notes; also two enclosures in long hand, seemingly letters from two different persons purporting to have psychic ability, written to Wilkins; also a two-page typewritten letter from him. (This last seemed surprising to me as I had not thought of his having a typewriter in the far north.)

At the time I picked up the letter at the Club I seemed to encounter George Ford, a theatrical producer member, who wanted to talk with me about something and I recall being annoyed as I wished to get away and go over the material.

Wilkins' letter contained report on some matters not referred to in news accounts—having a bearing on my impressions—and began with an apology for his inability to cooperate more fully, telling of his having been harassed by a multitude of details, "always something coming up to interfere." Unusual, unparalleled conditions in [the] north this season [are] also accountable for Wilkins not having the free time anticipated to give to the tests.

Specific information and comments in this interesting letter almost come back to me in my conscious state but cannot quite recall.

Somewhere in there floats the name of "Cleveland" and man's name, "Hooker," as though spoken—and having some business connection with Wilkins.

After examining this potential material, I seemed to find myself with Wilkins and observed him to be very grave of face—and not optimistic about the possibilities of his next flight. He said to me, "If anything should happen—if I shouldn't return—I would like Lady Wilkins to receive $10,000 a month." I had a vague feeling of some financial understanding with the Russian government with regard to pay for his own services—or some assurance given in the event of fatality that his wife would be taken care of.

Then Wilkins handed me a large bottle, dark blue in color, like the bottles containing oil at the gas filling stations, and it seemed half full of some dark liquid. He said to me, as he gave me the bottle, "This is to be buried with me."

I got the feeling, when he said this, that he had run out of fuel, the plane having lost its bearings in bad weather, and had made a forced landing, or that his oil line had become clogged or frozen.

The most singular part of the impression was Wilkins' seeming sense of finality and preparation for what he considered the inevitable.

In my conscious state of mind I have never had any apprehension concerning Wilkins for I have such complete confidence in his mastery of conditions relating to his flights. This, therefore, came as something of a shock.

I record the above dream consistent with my resolution to write down everything that comes to mind relating to Wilkins. What the causative forces behind this strange dream are, I cannot fathom. All of it seemed very real—and particularly my experience with Wilkins—just as if we were actually together.

New York
January 17, 1939

Last night I had another vivid dream that seems to have been related to some "incarnative" experiences. I was so moved by it that I awakened sobbing, the pillow wet with tears.

It seems that I was living again some moments that were mine in quite a primitive age, when humans traveled in tribes and fought one another with clubs for domination. Men had an animal-like regard for one another; respect was created only by fear of brute force; even supposed tribal friends or flesh-and-blood brothers were suspicious of one another, jealous and greedy. Constant physical combats ensued for possessions or command of followers in the tribe. Individuals were bludgeoned, severely beaten, or killed.

I was able to recognize the five Morrow boys, sons of my Uncle Arthur Morrow, my mother's brother, who were born and brought up in my mother's home town of Marion, Indiana. Lowell, Kenneth, Lawrence, Owen and Gus—all were tribal members—and my own brother Edward (now deceased) and my other brother, Arthur (I being the oldest in this life)—all were in these primitive scenes. (My middle name is Morrow, Mother's maiden name.)

Edward was least combative of all and avoided all conflicts where he could. He was beset often, without cause, because of his keeping aloof. I was repelled by the constant battling but had to fight in self-defense—and no doubt did my share of battering and killing.

The occasion which moved me greatly was a terrific tribal battle in which many were injured—and killed.

Understanding seemed to have come to me in that experience. I saw clearly the futility of such a struggle to gain human ends—the need for the expression of real brotherhood and love for one another.

I made impassioned pleas to the assembled tribes, with many of their members—those I knew and could recognize amongst them—for them to give up their warlike pursuits.

I can see them yet, staring at me with their strange-shaped heads, which did not admit of too-much intelligence, such as monkeys or gorillas stare at humans, as though trying to make them out, to comprehend.

In some faces was a dawning light of understanding; in others a dull, sullen expression. But all were moved in strange ways by my plea because I was *one* of them, and had apparently felt some deep urge within me that they *hadn't* felt or *couldn't yet* feel, because their bitter experiences —the law of the primeval in them, the struggle for survival of the fittest—had smothered a consciousness of any higher laws.

As I was awakening from this experience, vaguely conscious that I was crying in my sleep, and with this scene receding from me, there came a flash of another scene and a totally different type of advanced civilization, where I was making this *self-same plea*—for brotherhood and understanding between the peoples of the world—on a much broader scale, and these *two scenes seemed to fuse*, as though being part of the *same keynote!*

Then came the flashing consciousness that both these "incarnations" were *impinging on my present moment,* that I had come back into this life in an effort to bring greater understanding of themselves and their fellow men to the humans alive today, who were alive in other ages in which I had lived; and this was the reason that I, in my poor way, had been so profoundly interested in studying the hidden powers of mind and trying to discover the laws behind the operation of the human consciousness.

I was impressed, too, that I had a "karmic" relationship to these two experiences, and that—but for my having progressed further than many of my associates in the primitive experience—I should have been born back into this life, in the Morrow family, as one of Arthur Morrow's sons, my identity being distinct.

Even so, the law of attraction was such that I was born into this world through Arthur Morrow's sister, my mother, Mrs. Alcinda E. Sherman.

I have never felt closely drawn to any of the Morrow boys. They are more on the physical than the mental side, every one of them, and their development has been on the physical—the plodding, unimaginative, mechanical path of life, working largely with the hands.

As I was unable to save my brother, Edward, in *this* life from meeting with a fatal experience, so was I unable to save him then, from being beaten and killed by his primitive brothers. I may even have had some connection with this—that part is vague. (Edward died in this life at the age of 11, from injuries sustained in fall from a tree in our front yard. I had a premonition that this was going to happen that noon, and warned Edward not to climb any more trees, resisting an impulse to offer to buy him off by giving him a nickel on his promise not to go up in trees. My regret since then has been keen, although this strange force we call fate had perhaps marked Edward for passing at that time. His death had a profound and moving effect upon me and brought instant maturity.)

It is worthy of reflection, this feeling that has come to me, through this unexplainable dream experience, that what the soul has gone through, in all of what we consider to be the past, could be brought to the surface *if* we but knew how to *strike the keynote!*

For instance, my deeply rooted desire, born of past experience, to cause mankind to realize the futility of physical struggle against itself.

I attempted to put this message across in my picture, *Are We Civilized?*, dramatizing man's inhumanity to man throughout the ages. I have been devoting all my time and thought that I could spare, to a study of mankind and the effect of wrong and right mental attitudes upon individuals as well as the masses.

In this study I have been seeking the fundamental answer to the world's ills, and this dream makes me see more clearly my purposes in life—why I have had this *driving urge* since childhood.

We are driven into higher and higher development through our bitter experiences being the result of our own greed and ignorance.

Could we but strike the right keynote, it would bring up harmonics along the entire life line of our soul's experience. When a keynote is struck, vibration extends from the present moment of our conscious entity back into the so-called past and simultaneously into the so-called future.

Events truly cast their shadows before, and the shadows are as real, potentially, as the events!

New York
February 12, 1939

Last night, between twelve and one o'clock, as I was about to drop off to sleep, I had a vivid vision in my mind's eye. I was conscious, keenly aware of what I was seeing, in an entirely relaxed state. As nearly as I can describe it, I seemed to see a motion picture of a past civilization taking place in consciousness—only more real than a motion picture and three dimensional!

I found myself active in the construction of the Great Pyramid in Egypt. In a few flashing seconds of time, I saw myself superintending the loading of great stones upon specially constructed barges at a distance of five hundred miles or more from the site of the pyramid.

These stones were then transported down the river Nile and through a specially built canal by thousands of slaves or workers who had hold of thousands of ropes, attached to these barges. These workers ran along specially built runways on both banks of the canal, pulling the barges at incredible speed considering human manpower. They were relieved by thousands of fellow workers at different points along the route, the original workers then returning to their starting point to bring down the next loaded barge.

At the site of the pyramid, I now watched the great stones being put into place, high above the desert sands. I saw huge platforms on wheels, pushed and pulled by hundreds of humans—brought along on special tracks.

These platforms were rolled out onto *mammoth elevator lifts*, the shafts sunk into the ground *for as deep a distance as the pyramid was to be high!* Yes, even deeper.

And through certain powerful lifting devices, these elevator tubes would rise higher and higher into the air, beside the pyramid structure, until they reached the level desired, when these huge stones were rolled off on their platforms, onto scaffolding runways and taken to the exact spot designated for them.

My impression is that there were four elevator shafts, one on each side of the pyramid, sunk great distances into the ground. The elevators were lowered to the earth level when empty, awaiting the next lifting operation.

The area around the Great Pyramid, for some miles, seemed to swarm with antlike humans, feverishly busy, under armies of foremen, cursing and sweating—but all knowing precisely the part they were playing in the building of this enormous structure which was to stand the test of time.

It seemed to me that certain knowledge and control of gravitational forces was a help in this construction—but manpower was a tremendous factor.

I do not recall or ever having heard or read a supposition that these huge stones were transported to the pyramid site through a specially constructed canal. I should be interested if scientists could determine the possible existence of these great elevator shafts, some traces of which might still be found, far beneath the earth's surface.

I have done no reading or thinking in recent years that even suggest the pyramids.

New York
February 22, 1939

At 5:30 o'clock this morning, having spent a wakeful, painful night, due to the stomach disturbance that has been plaguing me, off and on, for months, I suddenly started to doze off and had the sensation of being in *limitless space*. Above and beneath me was an awesome void. There was no sensation of falling but a vital wonderment forced its way into my consciousness:

"Can there be any up or down in the universe?"

With this wonderment came an inner feeling that the answer existed coincidental with the question, that it was even then trying to express itself through my mind. I was so physically weary that I tried to throw these impressions off but they persisted and I finally got up, being on the cot in my study, picked up pencil and paper, and wrote the following at *high speed*:

There is no up and down. The universe extends in all directions from an endless succession of equa-centers. These centers are superimposed upon one another and synchronized with the center of every being in the cosmos so that each thing—animate and inanimate—is equi-distant from the equa-center or core which is forever expanding in an eternity of space-time!

The illusion is that the universe has one center at some fixed point in space is due to man's finite concept. Actually we are all at that center through our at-one-ness with the creative elements manifesting in us.

There is naught in the universe but a center; there could only have been one focal point, not as Mankind thinks of focal points, but when it is said that "God is not in any one place but everywhere"; and when Christ said, "Where my Father is, there I am also," it is meant that the most infinitesimal expression of our inadequate concept of God is centered in His Being—the bosom of the universe.

The *forms* of this expression are as infinite as the radiations from this center and the movements of this center are always circular.

Our bodies are whirling in their own molecular space, following the vibratory pattern set up at the moment of conception when the new energies were individualized, permitting the union of our identities which *themselves* are revolving around a spiral center, taking on higher speeds of vibratory revolution and demanding, as they do so, more and more refined cellular houses for our habitat, made necessary through our increasing awareness and comprehension of the God force in action.

We cannot die out of the universe any more than we can be born out of it. We could not have helped our being, since all that IS has always existed and no-one can conceive anything that is not. Nothing can ever be less than it is, though it can constantly alter its form.

Up and down in the universe—heaven as an imagined state *above* and hell as an imagined state below—all these are false and childish concepts.

The entire universe is *inside ourselves* and this is the mystery of BEING. We are searching through telescopes and microscopes for the center of all things in some remote place from whence all energies flow.

God said, as the Bible symbolically reports, "Let there be light," and there *was* light. But where and from what place came the voice of God?

The union of centers or concentric relationship of all things establishes a center of balance that accounts for what is termed "gravitation." It is the force that gives to all matter a pulsation.

The voice of God is then the infinitely varying wavelengths of this pulsation expressing forever-now in the infinite forms of worlds and stars and suns and all things and creatures thereon.

Up and down? How can there be an up and down to a center? Heaven and hell, as fixed localities, are non-existent; but AT-ONE-NESS with God—the universe—is the GREAT REALITY!

New York
June 10, 1940

I seemed suddenly to be in the presence of Laurie Bowen, boyhood friend of mine in Traverse City, Michigan, who had moved to Canada and joined the Royal Flying Corps there, giving his life in the last world war.

Laurie was in uniform and appeared eager to impress me with some vital information:

"Harold," he said, facing me directly and looking in my eyes as though concerned lest he not be able to reach my consciousness completely, "We have been trying to get this knowledge through to the world for years. There is a secret group in Germany, a band of at least a hundred who represent the strategy board or *brain trust*.

"These men are the leading scientists, inventors, chemists, technicians, military geniuses and *all-around* authorities in the country. They are kept in fortified seclusion, their every want satisfied in magnificent underground quarters in Berlin, containing industrial plants, laboratories, of every description, radio communication centers and every device and equipment for enabling this board to follow the progress of the war on every front at all times of the day and night.

"The theory behind this board is that the brains of the country need to be protected in a place removed from the terrific heat of battle where every development may be followed impassively, uninfluenced by the emotional stress and strain of leaders on any sector at the front who might be over-influenced by happenings and vision and reason so clouded as to make the wrong moves or decisions.

"All responsibility for the conduct of Germany's destiny rests with this board. Through an amazing communication system the decisions are made known to the general staff in the field and the coordinating arms of air, tank, infantry, artillery and naval forces concentrate action at whatever point or points is considered most strategic at the moment."

As Laurie spoke, *I seemed to be taken* to this underground headquarters, having the sensation of being in an immense, brilliantly-lighted corridor with high white walls on which were encased, under glass, great maps of all the different countries in the world. They were elaborate in detail with every conceivable military object located thereon and last-minute changes specified. These were *working maps*, but *opposite each*, on the other side of the corridor, was *another* map with the marked-out plan of action and the ultimate aims of Germany concerning that country which had been prepared years before!

This enabled the military strategists to know or recall, at a glance, the plan they had devised for the conquering of this particular country and to check the actual progress being made in that direction on the *working map*, directly across therefrom. I was impressed that no such system of detailed planning for war and for world domination had ever heretofore been conceived.

This strategy board, representing collectively the power of Germany, can then—through leaping abreast of every development, national and international—send out orders to agents in every country, starting agitation in Fifth Columns here, holding it up there, jockeying all their lines of attack to synchronize with the pressure Germany's armies are exerting on the field.

I was given the impression that Mussolini's apparent stalling was nothing of the sort. He is in the hand of his military planning board, subject to their orders, and will only move when they give him the word. Italian and Russian officers or representatives are guests of this German executive group but are actually hostages for the duration of the war, and should either Italy or Russia renege on her promises, those men's lives will be forfeited to preserve the secrets they now share.

I vaguely recall seemingly miles of underground rooms and passages, all strongly guarded and absolutely concealed from the knowledge of the unsuspecting rank and file of Berlin. Many Germans, now thought dead, having disappeared mysteriously some years ago, are alive and at work in these quarters.

Laurie told me, seemingly, that unless the location of this secret hiding place could be discovered and destroyed, together with the brilliant men who control and direct Germany's destiny, there would be little that could be done to prevent her conquering of the world in the due course of time, in conjunction with her present allies.

Hitler, outside coordinator of all the plans and movements that are perfected by the inner body, does not issue an order that has not been checked through the group. He would be lost were this powerful alliance of brains annihilated.

This system has been devised to prevent any disaster in the field, such as the possible capturing or killing of commanding officers, from deterring or destroying in any way the effective operation of German forces on any or all fronts.

In this manner, war can be carried on through what amounts to remote control, with the plan of battle communicated to all fronts daily, even hourly, and those in charge in different sectors simply following through.

This strategy board is in session 24 hours of every day, one third of its number asleep at all times but two-thirds on the job, awake and alert to every kind of happening anywhere in the world which may have an effect on, for or against Germany.

It is as though these men are sitting before a giant chess board, commissioned to develop all the checkmating answers to any moves that may appear, no matter from what countries they may come.

All strings are pulled in accordance with a pre-arranged plan and the designed result of each move is known in advance. The knowledge of human psychology and how to outwit, mislead or intimidate leaders as well as masses of different countries is profound.

Germany has thus, under Hitler, perfected a system such as the world has never seen, capable of cutting through all red tape and translating ideas and plans into action almost instantaneously in any part of the world.

Unless those countries opposing Germany can so organize themselves as to move with like speed, they are destined to go down in crushing defeat. Nothing can compete with such highly synchronized, organized power and the crystallization of all national resources in addition to the most brilliant minds in all Germany.

Britain and France, at present, have no national unity or planning board comparable; no well-mapped plan of attack or defense against such a deeply plotted and highly geared system.

Any baffling development in the way of war weapons or resistance that German forces may encounter becomes the immediate problem that this strategy board *must* solve. Since it is comprised of all technical minds, the solution is theoretically possible in this group and a specific answer developed. If it requires new inventive genius to counteract, these forces are set in motion.

It seemed to me that Laurie tried to reveal the location of the heart of this underground headquarters. He took me before a great map of Berlin and pointed to a section *on my left and a little above the lower half* as about the spot.

I got the impression of this spot being covered by an enormous building or group of buildings, comparatively new. One of the buildings, easily a block or several blocks square, appeared to have columns or pillars on three sides. The grounds or driveways about this structure were paved and landscaped, concealing from ordinary eyes the fact that all were highly fortified. I was impressed that the roof and walls of this building or buildings were of special thickness and design, built to withstand terrific bombing as a means of protecting vital underground chambers and living quarters.

As these impressions faded, I seemed to find myself facing Trev Carver, an old friend of Laurie's. I asked Trev if he had seen Laurie and he said, "Yes," that Laurie was "staying with him" for a few days, giving his child some special instruction. I got the impression that Trev's child had been a soul Laurie knew before incarnation as Trev's child and that Laurie was keeping in touch for world reasons, knowing the destiny the child had to fulfill.

I recall now that I was impressed with the fact that many who comprise this strategy board have lived for years in foreign countries and speak the native tongue of these countries, possessing an intimate knowledge of conditions and peoples there, so that authoritative information can be gotten from them whenever a situation arises without the necessity for going beyond the members of the board. This gives to those directing Germany's destiny an enormous advantage and facility.

The impressions just recorded were most vivid and my feeling of having been somewhere in company with Laurie is also quite real.

Diary   *New York*
February 17, 1941

After receipt of the second letter from Harry J. Loose, I made my first effort to assume a receptive state of mind and to invite impressions from or about him.

I stretched out on my cot, relaxed my body and turned my thoughts inward. I remained in this receptive state until about 11:45 a.m. EST, from about ten minutes after eleven.

As I opened my eyes, I saw, distinctly against the wall in front of me, next to the door, the outline of a pink rose, with green stem and leaves, as though it were a color picture or print.

To make certain it was not inner vision, I shut my eyes and the rose disappeared. I opened my eyes again and its image was still there, flat against the wall, larger than natural size, and next to the framed words of Fra Giovanni which have meant so much to me.

This is the first time, in my recollection, of ever having had such an experience. It caused me to wonder if this were an experiment, that some mind or intelligence was trying to determine if I were ready or could receive such impressions or images.

2

First Ara Messages

May 1941

Harold Sherman to Harry Loose   *New York*
May 6, 1941

Friend Loose:

    I have set aside a time roughly between eight and nine o'clock each morning for a session with my Comforter. This morning the attached material seemed to come through. It is based upon some truths you revealed to me and I am a bit self-conscious and over-sensitized about it. You see, I am so desirous of not permitting any "coloring" nor letting my imagination enter in, and gaining knowledge direct from a Higher Source, unpolluted. I will need, eventually, the proof of sight and actual sensing of Higher Intelligences as confirmation. Not that I doubt, but I am thinking in terms of the world and my ability to testify that these things are so. I know they are so, because I have experienced them. This has been my procedure in my stumbling way through this life. . . .

May 6, 1941

Before the Iberian was I am.

    Back in the early beginning of things my Spirit moved in the gaseous vapors of earth. Dispatched as I was from the bosom of the Great Intelligence with a host of other developed souls to bring light to the dark corner of this His seventh and last universe.

We brought with us the vibratory essence of all that was needed to create a new first life planet and this area in space-time became a new magnetic center for the play and interplay of universal forces in furtherance of the incomprehensible scheme of the Great Intelligence.

I moved behind the crystallizing and solidifying of these forces—the higher self of me—then responsive to the direct orders of Him who was giving expression of Himself through me.

And all would have been well had not certain parts of Him, given dominion over the creation of this world, become intoxicated with the power given into their hands. Through exercise of *their* will and not *His* will, lower forces were given power and control in the birth of this planet and the Great Intelligence, holding all responsible for this great mistake and error, issued the command that those who were here in the beginning should remain unto the end of such time as the great mistake might be rectified through all forms of life and manifestations which He had destined to occur.

Thus, I am as old as the planet Urantia in Him and grieve in my higher self for the cosmic severance of those long ago Intelligences from the following of His plan.

But now my spirit rejoices, for the illumination has come that I am near the parting of the ways when I will be divided from all that has gone before and taken unto another dimension once I have fulfilled this, my last mission upon earth, where all that has long been denied will be added unto me, yea—all that He had intended should be mine from the beginning.

And the mystery of my Being shall be made known as well as the mystery of Martha, that other half of me, contained also in Him, both of us a gift to each other that His work might be made manifest through us.

This little glimmer of knowledge given to me more as a test from my Comforter who signs himself "ARA"—if my poor receptacle of thought has interpreted the word-sound correctly.

Addendum

An elucidation of this meditation came to me following the sitting;

That the army of Intelligences sent to create this world had changed the plans of the Great Architect and had erected a structure containing fundamental flaws to be passed down through the centuries, necessitating a rebuilding job under direction of higher forces in conflict with lower forces wrongfully given power over elements they should not have controlled.

Once the planet Urantia had been given material form it was impossible to correct these flaws except as they were worked out and expiated by those responsible for the great mistake involving all life and happenings on the earth.

God, the Great Intelligence, in His compassion, has permitted those who brought about this great mistake the opportunity for redemption and has left the door open for all humanity to find its way back to Him.

It is our purpose to help open this door and reveal this light to Humanity which was plunged into darkness by the great mistake so long ago.

On the Super Chief en route to Los Angeles[1]
May 15, 1941

If you stand in the sight of God, you cannot see, nor do you want to see.

He sees for you.

When *His* sight becomes *your* sight, you can perceive all things with him.

---

[1] Harold was traveling to Hollywood to work for one month on the screenplay for *The Adventures of Mark Twain*, produced by Jesse Lasky for Warner Bros.

Then it is that you know that your soul is encased in a flesh garment. And then only you can put it aside as a cloak which, while serving, *binds*.

You have not seen the universe as it is until you attain God's sight.

Your earth vision is limited by the other cloak of Time and Space. But God's vision puts aside this cloak also and lets you stand in the presence of all knowledge in which Time and Space are swallowed up.

Behold, Time and Space now seem without you. A little while and you will know it exists within.

You see but the reflection of things, as one looking outward upon himself.

But, when possessed of God's sight, the reflection, which is illusion, vanishes.

To see with the spiritual eye as compared to earth vision, is as though you have been asleep for an eternity and seen nothing.

But now you are looking within the boundless heart of God, beyond all outward manifestations, wherein all returning and awakened souls find Peace and Wisdom which passeth understanding.

This will suffice.

On the Super Chief
May 15, 1941

The right hand of God and the left hand of Man.

Do not let the right hand know what the left hand doeth, for the left hand sinneth in the ways of man while the right hand reaches always towards the heavens and shields the spiritual eyes as they scan the skies of man's boundless opportunities in God.

The right hand is God's guide to man. There are always two choices in every act in life and the right hand of God can be in every one if we attune our wills to His.

When we do not, the left hand of our own desires reaches out and takes from us the feast that God has set before us, which we, temporarily blinded, do not perceive.

Watch your left hand, therefore, that it sin not against you and against Him who loves you but who cannot make His love manifest unless you lift your right hand up to His!

Herein is a great mystery, that man was made in the image and likeness of God and yet is divided into the left and right, having two sides to him.

In the beginning it was intended that these two sides should be as one but the flesh arm of man found pleasure in earth things alone, forgetting the arm of the Father.

When you clasp your hands to pray you speak symbolically your desire to join both sides of your nature—the left and the right hand of God.

Then it is that you sense the presence of the Comforter who comes close to you during this handclasp.

When the left hand finds its way back to the right hand of God, then the wanderer is nearing home. He comes once more within the hearing of God's voice who speaks only when the flesh side of man is subdued.

Today rulers of men have perverted the right arms of humanity. They have caused these right arms belonging to God to be raised in salute of everything vile and unholy. For this the blind and misguided must pay.

But the right hand of God is again being raised in this world by His disciples in whom He moves and has His being.

Keep your right arm then subservient to His will and His greater strength will make of your left arm a right arm also, that you may be purified to do the Father's work.

Your Comforter has spoken.

Hollywood
May 18, 1941; 2:20 p.m.

Today are you to meet with one who has been with you from the Beginning.[2]

Long is the way you two have traveled together, side by side as spiritual selves through countless times divided in body.

A veil is about to lift between you that you may stand in the illumination of your own real selves, darkened these many earth lives by your services in the flesh.

This joining of your forces in the flesh is being permitted that the one going on may leave with the one remaining here yet awhile the illumination which is his, that where he is you may be also, never more alone in the doing of thy Father's work, now closing in this last day and cycle of Urantia.

For the day of this earth shall not be as long as the long, long night thereof, since the Father has other plans for those whose feet have found the way and is leading their footsteps elsewhere, while the unenlightened ones still remaining shall be changed by the fiery heat of such cataclysmic human experience as Urantia, in all its awful history, has never had come upon it.

But this is only the necessary end for which a sad, mistaken beginning was made—and you are to be found serving in that time, letting God's voice speak through you, with the ears of a hungry multitude drinking in your words of true inspiration and wisdom, given you from on high.

You have come West as the first great step in your novitiate and here, as you sit, so seemingly alone, are gathered a host of fellow workers from Higher Planes who will be greeting you in the handclasp of Harry J. Loose, the Tree Planter[3] of old—and

---

[2] Harold was to meet with Harry Loose for the first time since 1921.
[3] Harry Loose told Sherman that as hybrids they had served together in a previous life, Sherman known then as "the Iberian," in a land that later be-

lo, be it known that you are the sapling he has planted which is to bring forth good fruit—fruit of the spirit, blessed and purified through the blood of fleshly sacrifice and devotion to the nameless cause—a cause to which your two souls have been so long, so *very* long committed.

For the one, there will come release for higher work in good and shortened time. For you also will come release of Spirit and of Wisdom that you may spread your branches to cover the reaches of the stalwart tree so soon to be transplanted for work in other realms.

Great joy and peace be with you both, on this, a most eventful day in your long pilgrimage back to the Father.

The homeland is in sight.

The host, surrounding you, have spoken.

Hollywood
May 21, 1941

Those who wait for a God to appear, who say God has not made Himself manifest to Man, are sleeping in the blindness and ignorance of the flesh. They have denied Him from the first and will not recognize Him, nor be recognized by Him, at the last.

Infinite Intelligence sustains only that part of itself which reflects it and, after a time, withdraws such sparks of expanding identity as do not ignite with the elements in outer manifestation nor tend to elevate through exercise of the Spirit, the forms occupied.

For the Way, in Higher Dimensions, divides and those souls or individualized segments of the Great Intelligence who

---

came known as Egypt, Loose wrote, "It was a fleshed appearance, in which the Iberian was an older earthman than I. The experiment and service was for a period covering a normal life range of the time and had to do with the introduction, propagation, and transplanting of trees and other vegetation in the-then land which at that time surrounded a great sea which is now the Sahara Desert." After this, Sherman often referred to Loose as "the Tree Planter."

pursue evil, do so to their own destruction and ultimate annihilation, even if it should require the obliteration of worlds and planets.

God is Infinite Intelligence in motion and any forces, given free and independent movement within certain realms, that elect to move counter to the Godward movement, provoke cataclysms in various parts of the universe, but alter God nor His incomprehensible plan not at all!

The still small voice is Man's connecting link with Higher Intelligence. It can be heard amid a Niagara of worldly sounds by those who lift themselves in thought and act above the world.

Whosoever will so do, hears the music of his own Being. Such a one can never again be torn apart by wrangling discords of this sorry earth. He rests secure upon the bosom of the Intelligence he *is!*

3

Hollywood

September 1941

Hollywood[1]
September 3, 1941

It is true, as the Tree Planter has said, that you are an Old Soul. Your original progenitor came from the planet Herma, a thousand billion miles from Urantia. His mating with a fleshed one of earth imparted to you an intermingling of forces which have tormented, baffled and inspired you throughout your long imprisonment here. Your awesome sensing of the infinity of Time and Space, which has all but engulfed you, has been due to the magnetic pull of your progenitor who yet bears a responsibility for the mistake which brought you into being, partaking of more than earth, yet less than the full next dimension—a hybrid[2]—as the Tree Planter has said.

---

[1] After an interlude in New York, Harold returned to Hollywood to continue work on the *Mark Twain* screenplay, this time driving west with Martha and their two daughters, starting out on July 22 and reaching Hollywood on August 17. During the next few months they visited Harry Loose every Sunday.
[2] Harry Loose introduced the subject of hybrids in one of his letters: "Way back in the beginning of things on this particular planet, a grievous "mistake" and partly an "accident" so happened together that its aftereffects affected a great number of minor intelligences on this present first, or beginning, dimension, which left them earthbound here, unable to advance. They

You have sought always to understand and to know, and in many lives this wisdom has not been denied you, yet the knowledge has only made more clear the path that you must journey, in company with your brother hybrids, on the quest toward liberation through service.

The Great and Eternal Father eventually rectifies all mistakes made by his erring children as He permits them origin and progress, as free agents, toward their inborn at-one-ness with Him. But once this mistake occurred, the Higher Intelligences, cognizant of it, decreed that the hybrids, as a creative experiment, should continue for a time to fulfill the duties originally intended alone for their progenitors, and remain in service to the evolving forms of human life here.

The hybrids, with their greater enlightenment, higher sources of inspiration and sensitivity, could be reached by Higher Intelligences having jurisdiction over the affairs of Urantia and commune with them during their temporary unfleshed periods between earth deaths and the times of re-enfleshment.

In this manner, while not primarily accountable for their state of being, these hybrids were called upon to render a greater degree of service than is ordinarily required of first-life creatures.

In the end, the reward of the Father will give spiritual recognition of this cosmic fact.

September 4, 1941

You have been with the developing race of human animals since the early beginnings.

---

are a sort of a "hybrid".... They are not fully in the next dimension nor fully in this [and] they cannot make full progress to the next dimension. For these many earth years, theirs has been a rather sad lot. They must have air and water as regularly as a fleshed intelligence.... These hybrids are fully organized, much the same as any earth order, and they have done, and are doing, much good here." Loose told them that hybrids would be fully explained in the Urantia Book, but when the Shermans began to study the papers they discovered that the hybrid material had been removed.

You and others like you have helped bring to man his growing knowledge of God and the true nature of the universe.

But you have suffered all the ills and imperfections of man, having the same body and being infused with the same spirit, yet the consciousness in you has been of a higher order because of the manner in which you were given first life.

You have always been dimly aware of God and have felt a kinship to some greater power beyond the earth due to your creative link with Beings of Higher Intelligence. Your full spirit has reached out, torn between the pull of earth conditions and the pull in you of those not of this earth.

You have sought happiness not alone in this world but in some vague unearthly state which you have sensed to be more real and lasting than your experience here. Always, however, your earth body has acted as an anchorage, dragging your soaring spirit back and causing you to realize that until this spirit could be quickened through complete mastery of all lower elements in you, the chains of your bondage could not be cast off.

You and your brothers and sisters in the flesh, so created, were automatically born into an order of service to all humans on this earth plane. Your earth fathers or mothers, having come to earth on missions of service and mating through the mistake with earth children, imparted to you this spirit of service.

This projection and dissemination of their spirits through offspring advanced you in the scale of first-life beings at the same time that it tied you to earth bodies until such a time in earth history when you might aid in bringing progressive release to all earth peoples.

That time is now close at hand and you are to be used as a seed planter that from the seeds of knowledge you sow, the consciousness of mankind may be raised and millions now groping in the flesh be awakened from their befogged dream and realize that they are at last free.

Ara, your Comforter, is with you.

September 5, 1941

Inspirational opening to Timothy 4, beginning 6th verse.

•••

The ministry to all mankind is near. Ages of earth time have been required to bring all consciousness involved here to the great changing point and the final dividing of the way.

You have known of this approaching moment and have been preparing to assume your part in it for many incarnations. This preparation has not been haphazard but all in accordance with a now incomprehensibly far-reaching plan developed in association with your hybrid brothers, yourselves in league with Higher Intelligences assigned to administer to the needs and problems arising out of the conditions surrounding human creatures on Urantia.

But you are soon to witness the flowering of thousands of years of service rendered toward the goal of liberating all humanity that you yourself may be liberated and start your homeward way.

Watch for the signs in and around you of the unfolding of the Plan and be you ready, day or night to respond.

This will suffice for this morning.

September 8, 1941

All those entrusted with the great and important earth missions must have learned submission to guidance for their protection and direction in the work undertaken. Without such guidance enfleshed souls are subject to the same ills of the flesh as those who are uninspired.

To you has been demonstrated what happens to the house of flesh when its occupant does not follow the voice of wisdom. Not once, but three times, as the cock crows. For you heard the voice within you, and have for years recognized it as an unidentified Higher Intelligence speaking to you, yet you wondered if the voice might, these times, be fused with your own physical forebodings of possible injury.

Today you no longer wonder. You *know* that the voice you heard was *my* voice, and you know you can henceforth hear it clearly and distinctly in your moments of need, if you *will*.

I have come a long way with you. I have seen you suffer much. But out of it I have seen patience and tolerance and fortitude grow. What you have had to experience in this life is as nothing to what you have undergone before. And yet much is to be required of you once your strengths of mind and body have been tested in this last earth life. You, more than most others, have never had time to waste. You have been about your Father's business for an uncomprehended period of earth years. You have failed on occasion—yes, as all have failed—but these failings have only quickened your resolution, made more firm your determination to fulfill in last degree the mission assigned to you, which is now approaching a glorious consummation.

Martha has been with you many times before—else, how could she have this understanding of you? And her destiny has been blended with yours in service, for the pathway has been lonely, fraught with pain and discouragement and temptations for loss of faith, when each has needed the other in order that both might cling to the knowledge and remembrance of the Father and your work in Him.

But now is come a day when much will be revealed, to you, and to the world. More and more will you give up earthly things of little moment, as the promise of eternal happiness becomes a living reality within you.

You are more receptive this morning.

September 10, 1941

St. Mark 13th chapter.

• • •

The time spoken of by Jesus is nearer at hand than the world realizes. Great and far-reaching evidences of the Father will be shown in support of the new and further word to be given the blind peoples of this dark planet. Only through catastrophe, man-invited and man-made, can man's sleep in the flesh be ended and his awakening to his true self and origin come to pass. The elect are awake; the blinders are being taken from their eyes that they may see God's purposes clearly and be about His business in a world of fleshly chaos.

But the time for all this is being foreshortened, the forces of change from an Old to a New order are awaiting the final mandate before loosing themselves. Your country is soon to go plunging into the maelstrom which will sweep all mankind into a whirlwind of economic, moral and physical destruction greater than any heretofore known.

Then may you know that the days for which your years have been lived are arrived. Then will your sealed orders be received. Then will your complete mission be revealed as well as the brothers engaged with you in the work of saving those who cannot save themselves.

The flesh profiteth nothing but the quickening of the spirit in the flesh meaneth much, for only in this way can God's presence be made manifest among men.

We are close to you this morning.

September 11, 1941

The quickened stage in the history of your time is at hand.

Watch the quickened speeding up of all movements between nations and peoples.

Watch the quickening of money exchanges.

Watch the quickening of fears and worries among the unprepared.

Watch the quickening of human hates and human greeds.

Watch the quickening of all things on this earth and, above all, the quickening of the spirits of men.

For out of this great approaching travail will come the greatest spiritual awakening ever to take place on this dark planet—an illumination transcendent in its effect upon even the most lowly.

For such a period and the participation therein have you been born and has your life been lived.

This, as Christ has said unto all, I say unto you: watch!

September 12, 1941

Millions of souls will soon be no longer interested in only the bread of earth.

There is even now a great hunger stirring in them for spiritual food. As they cry out in their hunger, they will be fed by those chosen ones who have been preparing a repast for them. The spiritual food will be placed upon the tables of their consciousness for assimilation. Truth will be available to all who seek it and their hunger appeased.

The Book of Urantia will be released at a time when the spiritual famine is reaching its climax, with the peoples of the world awakening to the realization that sustenance of the body is not in itself life; that life of the spirit is more precious and to be coveted than all the earth's transient wealth.

A great unrest dwells in the heart of humanity which dictators and armies cannot much longer restrain. This unrest will burst forth into a gigantic revolt against rulers and systems that would harness the spirit of man and sink him more deeply in the flesh.

Those who are being prepared to serve know that voices are to commence ringing in the wilderness of human thought, serving as beacon lights, so that, with recovery of spiritual sight, millions may be led out of flesh bondage into the first real freedom existent on this experimental planet since man came upon it.

Again I say—watch!—and bend your thought toward the planes from whence cometh the source of all spiritual power.

September 13, 1941

Event is soon to be piled upon event which will find the United States of America engulfed on several fronts in the desperately quickening stage of world conditions.

Deaths of some prominent Americans in war zones, the sudden death of a prominent national leader here and new assassinations of well-known peoples abroad will bring the seriousness of the unsettled times home to the people and cause them to realize as never before the instability and insecurity of man-made laws unsupported by the spiritual nature of man.

Sabotage will rise to unprecedented heights as hate-sated followers of different ideologies, the systems themselves misguided, will fanatically give their lives for worthless causes, only adding to the state of confusion and terror which must proceed mankind's awakening.

It must be said unto you again, in the light of these things: watch!

September 15, 1941

Man sleeps on the surface of life until his physical foundations are shaken by happenings of earthquake velocity. An inward shaking cracks and crumbles man's fleshbound way of thinking, opening up channels through which his real self may be reached.

In this quickening time real earthquakes in divers places will parallel man's inner trembling so that no place, within or without himself, will seem safe from devastation.

To you, and others in the flesh to whom a glimpse of the ultimate purposes and plan has been revealed, will be given the strength to stand while many about you are falling.

The house built without hands must soon be erected by all those who would survive these approaching times, otherwise millions, seeking shelter and finding no refuge within themselves, will perish.

It is this house that true knowledge of self and Man's promise of attaining at-one-ness with God will bring. In the Father's House are many mansions. Each part of Him is a room in this house, likewise a house unto itself containing a portion of God's indwelling spirit.

Your work will be the fitting together of these rooms in the mansion of humanity so that the long-dreamed brotherhood of man may appear as a great and wonderful highway, still afar off from the mansion but being builded brick by brick, nearer and nearer, until highway and mansion come together, each merging with the other.

Herein is the mystery of Time and Space, for Man, in the flesh, traverses a path in search of God, the Father, only to discover at the end of the road that God is beyond movement at the motionless center of the universe where all is still.

Then will Man comprehend the Biblical admonition, "Be still and know that I am God."

There is a movement behind motion, not now comprehensible to man. When Time and Space move together, that is Eternity.

Man imprisoned in the flesh can never be a part of this movement since all elements in his earth body are moving *through* Time and not *with* Time.

It is possible for intelligences in Higher Planes to observe wherein flesh movements are leading by looking along the Time dimension.

Since God, the Father, contains in consciousness all things, to *speak* with Him is to *create*. His voice brought us into being and we are now on the path back to Him from the outermost rim of first beginnings that we, at last, may greet God, the Father, in our *own* voice, singing His praises for being permitted to share the unutterable joy of conscious existence with Him, forever and forever.

September 16, 1941

You are surrounded by an organization of intelligences affording you protection against the forces that would operate against you, keeping open the channels necessary for you to express through and making available different individuals in positions of power and influence as instrumentalities.

Look for these new additions to your army of those who will provide, wittingly or unwittingly, the stepping stones you require to reach the objectives in human service designed for you.

As Martha was impressed, truly you will find, from henceforth, that you have been "entertaining angels unawares."

Learn to respond to the voice of guidance, even on occasions of seeming inconvenience, and you will be rewarded thereby. Great plans are in operation and much is in store for you.

September 17, 1941

There are seed planters who come to this earth with new forms of life. There are also "idea planters" who till only the soil of human consciousness. This soil differs greatly according to the grade of development, it is fertilized by human experience which enriches it so that the "idea planters" can drop finer and finer ideas for progress into it.

This is always done with the cooperation of the Thought Adjuster who stands guard at the portals of consciousness and who knows what the soil is ready to receive. Different individuals attract different "idea planters," themselves specialists in arts and sciences and subjects homogeneous to the soil of human consciousness contacted.

In this manner, just as those more advanced here help those less developed, so do higher developed entities, on missions of service, bring inspiration to those who reach out for greater knowledge in the sphere of their own interest. They are as air and water to actual soil, the essence of the idea or pattern of progress being absorbed by the soil of consciousness which nourishes the unfolding life expression and brings about fruition of many earth accomplishments.

But no ideas can be planted in the soil of human consciousness which it has not been prepared to receive. There are low-grade idea planters as there are low-grade peddlers of wares on earth. Low-grade seeds will not grow in too refined a soil.

Your soul swims in a creative sea of consciousness which eternally emanates from the Father or source of all things. Earth experience was designed to teach you discrimination, that from this creative sea you might crystallize in your life only the highest and best.

All manner of elements and conditions swirl about each individual soul, and unless he has learned to be still within his own center of being, the eddies of unwanted forces will drag him in.

You have seen how driftwood is sucked into a whirlpool, but the real river current runs on strong and true. So long as you keep swimming in this stream you will be borne along to finer and finer shores of realization. But see to it that you avoid enticing pools of stagnation whose movement, at times, is bewilderingly like that of *the* stream and yet is not free, forward going but round and round in the same vicious circle of non-progress.

Many are caught in this deceptive whirlpool and their development arrested while they revolve about debris of no value or importance. Eventually a soul-shattering experience breaks them loose and sends the debris flying but they are often dazed and lost and go floundering down the main stream again, unable to derive much of its beneficent influences because they have not learned how to *breathe in* what is meant for them as they find themselves immersed in the flow of creative energy seeking expression.

The tide in the affairs of earth is coming in. It will prove too strong for millions of humans now hopelessly engulfed in whirlpools of their own making. This tide will throw them up upon the barren beaches of their own soil consciousness when realization of their own physical and mental futility to face the ordeals of life rushes in upon them.

It is then that this soil, made virile by the putrefaction of dead and dying wrong ideas and concepts, is hallowed by the army of Higher Intelligences and made ready for the leaders of the new order on earth to plant "spiritual seeds" from which a transformed humanity will grow.

Do you begin to see now the harvest promised by the Bible, and what its significance is to be?

All life is creative force in motion, directed or undirected. When you have disciplined it, in and through your own entitized experience in the flesh, and have learned to respond to the guidance of the Father through His appointed servants, then you are on the upward path forever beyond the *reach* and *pull* of elementals.

September 18, 1941

Luxury is the wasting of earth time on idle pursuits. It is a luxury that no awakened soul today can afford to indulge.

... All those on missions here are weavers of a pattern designed and placed on the loom of Time long centuries ago. The strands of service are in their hands and must be woven into place so that God's handiwork may be completed on this dark planet. Day by day new brother weavers will be revealed to you and the strands pulled tighter and tighter until great portions of the pattern will become discernible and the results of your own labors reflected upon the heart of mankind.

The Master Spinner sits at his wheel and gathers all strands of service into a carpet upon which the feet of all human creatures may tread to spiritual salvation. Today all flesh is footsore, confused and weary, stumbling along an uncarpeted way. If you neglect the completion of your strands you bruise the feet of your fellow pilgrims.

A lamp has been given you that you may see your weavings more clearly. It has been filled with the oil of experience, and lighted by the fire of inner wisdom. This lamp will burn more brightly as you bend to the loom of service, and will cast a protecting glow about you as fire drives off the wild animals of the forest. For there will be many who will seek to destroy the weavers in whose flesh bodies the animal nature still runs riot. But they will be blinded by the light and held off.

Great power is being generated and soon you will hear the hum of the looms as all weavers bend to their tasks. It will be the sweetest music to your spiritual ears ever heard in this world of discord and it will sustain you throughout the period of chaos to come.

September 19, 1941

When great soul-quaking changes are about to occur on the earth plane, the planet itself trembles throughout its uttermost parts due to the devastating interplay of changing forces.

Every great earth cataclysm has come at a moment of fundamental disturbance in the consciousness of mankind. This will always be so, since the elements which respond to intelligence are affected as the tides by the shifting of the action of intelligence.

Unenlightened man can only see and judge the results of his misguided thinking through the punishing experiences he attracts to himself in his physical world.

The flesh body is of the earth earthy and registers, through its elements, the elemental changes taking place in nature. With the spirit in man quickening it is as though a more powerful electrical charge were being sent over many wires incapable of handling it.

Those who attempt to resist this quickening of the spirit in the flesh will find themselves short-circuited from all higher forces that might otherwise strengthen and sustain them through the days to come.

Man's heart will quake within him as the earth trembles under him. He will be caused to wonder at the signs in the heavens and in the earth and in the center of his own being—for he is at-one with all these things, yet has considered himself apart.

His residence in the flesh will avail him nothing for there is no place of safe retreat in the flesh house alone but only in the arms of the Father who claims his own through their free-willed recognition of Him.

At the proper time the power and the channels will be opened through which you, in company with your enmissioned brothers, may guide the footsteps of millions of souls who have been earnestly seeking the Path.

Be patient and prepare. The time is not afar off.

September 20, 1941

Are you watching? Even as you do, events are rushing upon events. The world crisis grows apace and no balance is to be found among men. Yet, even so, no thought is to be given to the morrow, sufficient unto each day will be your strength and your knowledge thereof.

The plan for this dark planet and its imprisoned peoples is being unrolled as a great scroll which has been centuries in preparation. Written thereon is the destiny of all, indescribably and incomprehensibly intertwined and yet readable to those whose vision has been lifted above the earth plane so that they can perceive the pattern woven by mankind itself.

Witness the inexorable forward rush of events in your own life as evidence that the way has been prepared. Unto you, more and more will be given as you open the channel of your instrumentality. The highway of service stretches before you, clear and straight beyond the mists of your developing consciousness.

Your seeking is over. You have found the road and it is moving under your feet, carrying you along two steps for every step you take. Forces are already reaching out to unite with your own force. A great circuit of world service is being closed, soon a great light will burst upon this dark world at a moment when all seems lost. You and your brethren are to provide the candlepower for this light, so hold yourself in readiness and know that all is well with you, that the house in which you dwell cannot be shaken for it rests upon the only unshakeable foundation in the universe.

Be of good cheer.

September 21, 1941

Through the agency of him who has served with you this long, long time there is being built around you a wall of power in the form of enfleshed and unfleshed entities who will protect, sustain and support you in the important work you are destined to undertake. Each day will carry its own evidence of this fact as new associations come to you and individuals with no outward seeming development reveal their spiritual attunement. Others, through influence brought to bear, will be caused to open up, that you may plant the seeds which will bear fruit for you as well as for themselves toward the goal of service you seek. Many will aid you, unaware for the time being of why they have been impulsed to do so, because you have touched a responsive something in their deeper natures with which they themselves are yet not too familiar.

You will commence to see now the purposes behind the long years of physical, mental and economic hardship and the power which these experiences have generated. To be patient beyond ordinary human endurance; to be understanding and tolerant when not understood; to be insensitive to pain of body or hurts of man; to know inwardly that all is well when all outward signs are to the contrary, and to remain unmoved and quietly serene in the face of happenings which to those uninitiated would seem cataclysmic—this is the development required of those who are to serve as humanity's balance in and through the approaching crisis.

You and the Tree Planter of old have prepared long and faithfully, with thousands of your brothers, toward this earth moment of spiritual travail which is now nearing. Each day is an increasingly priceless pearl in the string of Time. Let these pearls not slip unheeded through your fingers, each has a value to leave with you of far more than human worth. The Tree Planter knows whereof I speak.

September 22, 1941

The will of God and the will of man.

Countless earth years ago, when the animal body you now inhabit evolved to the state permitting union with Higher Intelligences, it possessed a will based upon the desires of the five physical senses. What the animal consciousness had found desirable to it, it willed to have. But this will was not tempered by wisdom nor disciplined by spirit. It was strong or weak in accordance with the decree of body energy, the ability of this body to generate power in any direction upon which its attention might be fixed. Progress was in the field of physical perfection alone until the body consciousness became fused with Higher Intelligence—an impartation from God.

This experiment in the development of earth creatures brought about immediate conflict since two beings now existed in one flesh.

Higher Intelligence, entering in, lost its remembrance that it had come from the Father but retained its upward climbing urge and demanded that the animal body subordinate its will to the will of the indwelling spirit.

But the animal consciousness sensed that this surrender of its own will meant loss of its identity in the flesh. For centuries this earth battle in man has continued, with the two wills contesting.

"Not *my* will but *Thy* will be done!" Many a weary soul has prayed, having conquered the animal consciousness at last, this animal consciousness being blended with the spirit and transformed, thus preserving its identity apart from the body in which it had first gained origin.

It is only then that the indwelling spirit has been able to recollect awareness of its at-one-ness with the Father, for the long residence in a flesh body has dulled sense perception.

Yet it has been the decree of the Great Intelligence that these earth creatures be lifted up, their corrupt bodies being given incorruption—but only as their animal wills might be led to voluntarily subjugate themselves to the higher indwelling will of the spirit.

Without the guidance of the higher will or intelligence, human creatures would have had nothing to distinguish them from the so-called lower animals which have not been animated by the God-Spirit in this sense. Man would not have survived. He would have become extinct as the dinosaurs and countless forms of earth life have become.

But, because, in this experimental world, the evolution of this earth animal, man, held greatest promise, it was granted that man, as a form and expression of the Great intelligence, should not perish.

Everlasting life with the Father has been assured through different states of progression beyond this earth plane but only after the soul resulting from this fusing of spirit and body has subdued and translated the lower elements of Being.

The will of the Father is ready at all times to speak through you when the will of your animal body has been made passive; ultimately experience demonstrates to the will of the flesh that the will of the spirit is not an enemy but a friend.

Gradually, as knowledge of the Higher Self comes to the Lower, the two wills become as one, and this is the marriage made in Heaven when at-one-ness with the Father is accomplished by renunciation of the human will and the long hold it has upon the entity that is *you!*

There is much more to this great and mysterious subject of the will but this will suffice for this morning.

September 23, 1941

The illusion of some mortals that they will escape the consequences of what is to come is based upon the false premise of self-indulgence.

Instinctively, intuitively, every soul knows that the end for which the fleshly beginning was, is near at hand. Nearness is not a matter of time but of condition. The great change has already come in the lives of thousands. It brings a peace and contentment and sense of security not of this world. You are just beginning to experience it. You cannot truly dwell with the Father until you have learned to still every fleshly impulse. This is accomplished through deep meditation and a uniting of your will with His. It is the only way in which you may overcome the will of the animal and gain the ultimate liberation you seek. Having overcome all things lower than yourself, your entity is then freed for the upward climb, not in distance but degree.

Millions are to be given this opportunity for advancement soon. It is now your preliminary duty to assist in the awakening of a few select souls who are being readied for service.

September 24, 1941

There have been moments in your life when you have sensed the great void of the past, when the awesome realization of what has gone before has almost suffocated your consciousness as a breath that has been withdrawn.

Time does not pass; it exists in layers and you evolve spirally through it on the flesh plane, never returning to the same layer. It is like the bands or rings of time in a tree trunk, the days of which are numbered, even as the days of your earth life with respect thereto.

You are the one who passes through the layers of Time, for Time, as such, does not basically exist. This outer world is conditioned universe and we are conditioned beings in it. If Time did not exist in layers we could not return to the same point on an ascending spiral and continue our advancement in the flesh.

Looking *down* through Time, through these layers, with developed inner sight, you could see civilization after civilization, the astral essence of it still in existence down to the minutest detail so that, once attuned, you could relive what has gone before by descending to that layer of Time.

Once, in what you called a dream experience, you were taken on a journey through Time with Martha and you came back with an incomplete impression of your experience. I was your guide, your *governor*, and the many *automobile tires*, as you described them, piled one atop the other, were the rings of earth experience you had undergone. You ascended, you remember, via an elevator to a certain level and you met people who talked a different language which you then seemed to understand. Do you recall that you had the feeling that people in each level existed entirely independently of the others on different levels and that they never had to leave these great buildings during an entire life time, that everything they wanted was there? They *could not* leave that level of Time for so long as they had been born into it, until they should be released to the next layer through death, the magic key to soul advancement.

All flesh elements must be left in the layer of Time to which they belong since the Soul or entity is the only part of man which progresses.

What you were shown you retained symbolically but without interpretation. You saw the real Martha devoid of flesh in the in-between state as she appeared at the organ and you felt the harmony of your two souls in the music to which she gave expression, so pleasing to your spiritual ears.

Souls of true affinity sing with the joy of Being. Everything in motion gives off sound, could we but hear. There is truly the music of the spheres; and there is the music of the soul, beautiful beyond words when two souls sing as one.

You were taken ahead in Time and shown a glimpse of the wonders to come which you only recall now with a faint glow of exquisite pleasure. And then, as you recall, you were put back to sleep in the flesh, while others were passing down the corridor of the layer of Time you were then in. When you awakened in your own layer of Time, you saw two of these entitles still standing beside your bed, now talking in a strange tongue, superimposed, for the moment on your flesh consciousness.

Full comprehension is not as yet yours, but one day you will be enabled to travel backwards and forward through the layers of Time and then much can be revealed which is now only darkness and a void to the present flesh body.

Ponder well on what has been written this morning.

September 25, 1941

A soul advanced in service on the earth plane has surrounding him a band of workers. He is helped more than he realizes through situations that might otherwise prove unsolvable or unbearable. More help is given as the soul evidences the deservability to receive help. And yet, no soul is deprived of its own initiative nor is anything done for it that it essentially must do for itself. But workers are paving the way along the lines of aspiration of the soul often years ahead of the expression or accomplishment on the earth plane.

It is all part of a picture or plan into which each enmissioned soul fits. You are not alone in your strivings. Higher Intelligences are as dependent on you in the fulfillment of their missions as you are dependent upon them in the fulfillment of yours. For this reason you must keep your channel of communication open that you may divine, more and more, your own soul's purpose in this life and the plan of service of which you are an integral part.

No "orders" can be received when the soul is immersed too much in fleshly things. When the telephone switchboard of your body is clogged with local calls, you cannot receive important long-distance messages from those who really count.

True inspiration comes from those in higher realms. It is in this manner that you also, on occasion, "entertain angels unawares."

4

Hollywood
October 1941

October 7, 1941

Events are rapidly shaping themselves which will strengthen your position with *Mark Twain* and open up new opportunities for you along the line of your real talents.

You already have evidence of support in your collaborator who is responding to your revelations of truth and will be associated with you when your real life work begins.

Watch for additions to the ranks of those who have been prepared to render service, and the forming of a strong band of men and women upon whom absolute reliance may be placed so that you may eventually stand against all resistance. Everything is proceeding as it should and only *good* will basically result as you move forward under guidance of your inner wisdom.

October 8, 1941

A storm area forms slowly, gathering all the elements from earth and sky.

In much the same manner, your own forces are collected through developing experiences in life until the day when you find yourself a definite power moving in a purposeful direction, capable of sweeping all before you in the way of opposition. Your movement is really spiraling like a cyclone, with your powers expanding from a center of dead calm wherein dwells your directing spirit.

Those around you feel your increasing power, are sucked in by it, caught up and carried along, adding their forces to your motivation. The lesser entities always seek strength through union with the greater. The magnetic attraction of the sun draws up particles of water from the earth which in themselves are not potent but which, when joined in vast numbers can rain down great life-giving nourishment over a wide area on this planet.

There is a constant, incomprehensible interchange of forces taking place; likewise a continual blending and linking of entities on missions of service. Many entities, not sufficiently developed, are used like the individual drop of water, unconscious of the service rendered, yet this service has brought progress to the entity.

It shall be given unto you to influence the lives of many entities through the increasing power of your own revealed wisdom and expression. Already your spiritual forces have revolved about the lives of many more thousands, yes, numbering into the millions of men and women, boys and girls, than you may consciously realize. You have touched their consciousness in a manner that has stepped up its vibration. Once influenced, these entities draw from you particles of inspiration and guidance for they have given you lodgment in their minds and hearts—not as an entity but as a force.

You are the stone which once dropped in the pool consciousness, continues to send forth ripples of inspiration and light.

Observe now the responsibility all leaders of mankind take unto themselves and the penalty many will one day have to pay for sending forth wrong and destructive influences.

Of two storms, approaching each other from opposite directions and meeting, the stronger will survive after a terrific clashing of the elements, ending by whirling the lesser up in it, changing its entire nature and path.

Just so will the forces developed by you and other enmissioned brothers in the flesh, rise up in a righteous storm to beat down the forces of darkness which are casting a cyclone pall over the peoples of earth. The elements are gathering for the titanic conflict and you have sensed their movement for years, being at times greatly disturbed thereby, for you had not then developed the power and wisdom to withstand the tempest.

You are now reaching a point wherein the sun will always shine for you while all is dark on earth, it will be your mission to bring this light through the clouds of despair hanging low over the misguided heads of millions.

Then will the true *rain*, not *reign*, of peace and understanding come. No earthly rule can bring it. But human creatures must absorb this spirit as the earth hungrily absorbs the falling drops of moisture, so that they become an actual part of the higher forces in operation.

This is the only way that advancement can come and lower elements transcended by fusing with the higher.

October 9, 1941

Do you not begin to see how the steps you have taken in life are leading up to the same path of service from different directions?

As it was revealed to you in brief, fragmentary glimpses, years ago, you have come along many arduous roads up to the present moment when *all* these roads are at last merging into THE path.

Within three years you are to be widely and favorably known, the subject of great discussion—a mighty *pebble* dropped in the pool of world consciousness, causing a tremendous stir therein.

Your powers of expression will then have been given full flow under the guidance you are now knowingly following so that your influence from public platform, press, radio, stage and screen will be enormous.

You have been given responsibilities and tested physically, mentally and economically by forces working in and through you, that you might be strengthened for the full mission ahead.

What would kill or bring about the collapse of an hundred men in the time to come will not touch you. It would have been no kindness to have possessed the talent without the developed *will* of execution. And *your* will, as the Tree Planter has indicated to you, has had to be merged with the Will of the Father which never compels but which is the strong right arm of the spirit forever. What is there to fear when such an arm supports you in the face of your earthly adversaries.

Events are rapidly falling into place to fill out your chart of service, soon you will see the whole plan laying out before you as you have inwardly known it from the beginning.

"Take up your cross and follow me," sayeth the Lord.

The fleshly cross is always hard—the *cross* between the animal and the spirit, which one day will be severed, thus setting the souls of mankind free. This is to be your field of service; plow deeply this field for it has been made fertile for the implantation of spiritual seeds.

October 10, 1941

The world crisis is moving swiftly along toward the United States' active participation in the war. Japan, as indicated in the paper reports, will touch off the spark in the Pacific in the hope of keeping America busy there while Germany brings increasing pressure on the Atlantic side as England now *really* has to fight for her life.

This struggle, as viewed from dimensions beyond, is rooted in causes which have their foundations deep within the human creature, tracing back to early beginnings of different races.

The end of this era is rapidly approaching amid great and incomprehensible turmoil of spirit. It is the last great battle being waged by the animal self of man for survival, it knows that it must ultimately surrender to the spirit which dwells within but is striving to prove to the residing soul that it is sufficient unto itself.

This carnal effort failing, the animal self then will implore that it be taken over by the spirit for its own salvation. This harmonious union of the lower with the higher selves of Being finally atones for the great mistake made in the long ago and gives back to all elements the properties and qualities and progressions originally designed and intended.

The striking of such a balance is not accomplished without cataclysmic happenings on the earth plane like a cauldron boiling over as all elements are refined, through the intense heat of human experience.

But there will be those who will be protected and remain unscathed through the seething human inferno to come. They are the new leaders of the God Spirit in man which will manifest itself at a time when the animal in man is running riot.

It has been written that the Great Intelligence would permit the animal in man to rule for a time to demonstrate to itself that it, alone, is not equipped to govern, nor to exist, without the indwelling spirit. This is the lesson earth life is supposed to teach, a lesson which evolving creatures here must learn.

Martha handwritten note   *after December 12, 1941*

December 7—Japs attack Pearl Harbor in surprise bombardment finding Navy totally unprepared.

December 8—Japs occupy Thailand and invade British Malaya

December 9—*HMS Republic* and *Prince of Wales* sunk by Japanese planes off Malaya

December 12—Guam captured by Japs

October 13, 1941

What you have seen and experienced in your long, long journey up to the present is not lost to you; it has only been withheld for a little while. Just as inner vision would be confusing to you if operative at all times on earth, so would the impingement of past life memories prove upsetting and bewildering in your daily rounds now. Much development must come before the veil can be lifted for the soul and he is permitted to look backward along the arduous path he has traveled.

You sink into the ocean of your entire life experience during sleep and, occasionally awaken with vague memories of indescribably beautiful adventures or the very reverse condition which you set down as a harrowing nightmare. Often these recollections have nothing to do with any experience undergone in this flesh body but reach back in time to some ordeal of the soul, some anguished mistake which has still left its mark in consciousness.

Just as the striking of a note will bring answering chimes from other equally attuned objects, so does a vivid experience in this life sound down through corridors of time, awakening all past experiences of like nature. These experiences may not cross the threshold of flesh consciousness in recognizable form, existing many times only as inexpressible feelings which seem to well up from the unfathomable depths of Being.

Your life is a symphony of experience. It is constantly being played upon by forces from within and without and the nature of your reaction to this interplay determines the degree of harmony or discord realized by your entity.

The ultimate destiny of your soul is the attainment of complete and absolute harmony through attunement with the

Great Intelligence. When this state of development is reached, you then receive the embrace of the Father and go not out any more as a part Him but remain *one* with Him in an eternal existence beyond the power of earth language to describe.

As you overcome fear and exercise faith, more and more can be shown you. Belief must come before revelation since belief shuts off all fleshly protests of the physical senses which have no capacity to sense other than earth plane experience, and opens the door to the faculties of the soul which can know all things, as it progresses, through wisdom sent by the Father.

Your Thought Adjuster stands guard at the gateway of your soul and will guide everything that you may wish to enter in, if you will counsel first before opening the gate.

Each soul must learn how to protect himself against the incursion of destructive forces since a flesh body that can be occupied by intelligence can also be preyed upon by other intelligences unless the inhabiting entity maintains control. You should be influenced only by Higher Intelligence—never by the low grade elementals—always seeking recognition or some vicarious, momentary association with the flesh. You must realize that you are surrounded by intelligence of inconceivable variety, directed and undirected, all in different stages of unfoldment. You are in the turbulent sea of life and your rudder is your Thought Adjuster. Keep your hand in His and all will be well.

October 15, 1941

Your animal self knows nothing, beyond this physical world. For this reason your soul is in constant conflict as it endeavors to make a receptive instrument of the body.

This is the cross your spirit has been called upon to bear these many incarnations because of the fusing of higher elements with the lower.

Fundamental processes of evolution—*upward reaching*—cannot be altered but the outward forms of life expression may be infinitely changed.

You, as a human creature, are occupying one of these forms in a state of evolvement. Without your directing spirit, animal forces would run riot. Witness what is happening all over the world to millions of enfleshed souls who have lost their hold upon the body. As rightful tenants of these houses of flesh, they are being ejected by the lower elements which rise up to dispute this tenancy due to the great mistake which was originally made.

(This is a big, a somewhat bewildering and a vital subject. We will continue it at another time.)

October 17, 1941

Consider a physical body not originally designed for the fusing of elements from higher dimensions, is it any wonder that the blending of enfleshed intelligences with evolving human creatures should have brought about confusion between higher and lower phases of consciousness?

Ultimately these struggling human creatures, under proper guidance, would have reached spiritual states of being commensurate to those occupied by the enfleshed Higher Intelligences. But this union of the two, due to the mistake in orders, involved both in what might be termed a karmic relationship.

These human creatures, once mated with entities from higher dimensions, possessed through their offspring on the earth plane a type of being never before conceived. The indwelling spirit, an impartation from the Great Intelligence, found itself imprisoned in a body containing elements much lower than itself in evolvement. The body consciousness naturally resisted the presence of a something which continually reminded or plagued it with an awareness of a destiny extending far beyond its physical limitations and the power of the body consciousness, in itself to comprehend.

The indwelling spirit, despite the fact that it represented a newly conceived soul, because its origin had come from Higher Sources, possessed a spirit body of its own. This spirit body, however, was chained to the physical and its higher faculties of sensitivity dulled or completely submerged by the manifestation of the so-called five physical senses on the earth plane.

Only rarely, when the physical body—through unusual passivity brought on by extreme fatigue or excitement—would let down the sensual bars of resistance, could the higher forces of the spirit evidence themselves.

The spasmodic demonstration of powers beyond the physical often served to awe-inspire or terrorize the physical consciousness of man which has never wholly understood the relationship and has rebelled against these powers, many times wrongly interpreted as "works of the devil."

There has remained a vague remembrance of the great mistake when powerful forces united with earth elements and brought about a psychic storm which has carried down through the centuries of time on this planet.

Once the fusion occurred, it could not be undone without bringing an end to the forms of life known as human creatures. This would have necessitated the withdrawal of that portion of the spirit already willed by the Great Intelligence and expressing itself through the individualizing entities resulting from this union. These developing entities had a God-given right to this identity since they had been in no way responsible for the error. And the only way that this identity might be preserved and developed now lay through repeated residence in the flesh, so that eventually nothing would be lost, either to the evolving consciousness of the human creature or that of the indwelling spirit imparted by its original progenitor from a higher dimension.

The only salvation for both types of consciousness contained in the same being then lay in subjugating and transcending of the lower self by the higher.

It has been impossible for the higher self to free itself from this physical body through which it has gained soul-developing experience and leave this lower self behind to which it has become karmically obligated.

The physical consciousness has clung only to what it knows or senses as reality throughout this long time, resisting the imploration of the spirit incarnation after incarnation, not realizing that its own liberation depends upon complete surrender to permit the higher self the exercise of powers far transcending the physical.

This accounts for earthbound souls, for all the vagaries of elemental and psychic manifestations so confusing to the mind of man.

Higher forces have been working all these countless years, striving to undo the myriad complications arising out of this mistake.

In the great ultimate, nothing will have been lost and what you have suffered will have become a crown upon your head. You are even now regarded with what amounts to envy by many Higher Intelligences who see an infinite value in the special experience that has been yours. And yet the road has not been easy, nor is it easy now. You, as an awakened soul, can now be reached and taught by Higher Intelligences assigned to help work out the problems on this experimental planet of Urantia.

And much is going to be required of you, just as much will be given. There are numberless entities, still prisoners in the flesh, who have not as yet been able to rise above their lower selves and to recognize their true kinship or identity. These souls need loving help and guidance.

October 19, 1941

Your physical eyes have beheld many past civilizations; your physical ears have heard and understood many languages of peoples long since disappeared from this earth; your physical senses have thrilled to scenes and experiences piled one upon another countless times over, leaving their impress upon your soul. Each time as you left your receiving instrument, the body, you took the record of this life experience with you. You took also this evolving consciousness of the human creature with you as *your link* to the planet Urantia upon which you became imprisoned through union of higher enfleshed entities with the developing human forms they had come upon earth to guide.

This lower consciousness of which your higher self is a part possesses the power to recreate itself in physical form. All physical life comes from the sea or fluid state. In this way are elementals fused, absorbing one another and yet retaining their identity in a new form.

You owe a great debt to this lower self for it has provided the bodies for your continuing experiences in this plane of life. As the influence of your spirit has made itself felt upon the lower self, you have been enabled to elevate your whole being.

Consider, if you will, an invader forcibly residing in your home. Then perhaps you can comprehend the age-old conflict between the lower self and your indwelling spirit and get a sensing of the enormity of the great mistake. Here, originally, were human creatures, setting forth upon the path of upward progression, having union among themselves and containing elements which they understood. Then came the day when unintended union occurred between higher enfleshed intelligences and these human creatures, bringing offspring containing the elements of both.

The self of the human creature, being aware now of the presence of a new and strange consciousness or entity within, resisted this consciousness as an intruder.

But the higher self, carrying a vague memory of its past glorious estate, would constantly cause the lower self moments of remorse for its carnal activities in the flesh. The lower self, striving to understand these weird feelings, felt between two seas, buffeted by external experiences and the inward tides of higher urgings.

The higher self knows that its only hope of release of the spirit from entanglement in the flesh must come through elevation and sublimation of the lower.

Oh, the unspeakable, the unutterably long, long battle it has been up to this present moment of awakening from this ages-old sleep in the flesh!

The Great Intelligence, mindful of the struggle of His creatures on Urantia, sent Christ, one of His highly developed Sons, to awaken the spirits of men. But the flesh in man rose up to repel and deny the Truth—and the Time was not yet.

Christ, as one of those originally associated with the great mistake, returned to earth on a mission to sacrifice Himself that the mistake might be rectified. Insomuch, He *did* die, as man has died, that man might eventually be saved.

Do you begin to see behind the veil now? Do you begin to sense your relationship to the indescribable void of the past? You have known, in many past civilizations, this same old story and you have, through the influence of your words and deeds, started many souls on the path toward liberation—just as you are to do again—in this life.

One day you will see the past as clearly as you see the present. It will stretch before you as a great plain or panorama and you will see an unbroken line, leading back, back, back into the dim beginnings of things on this First Life Planet.

"Be of good cheer!" said Christ, "for I have overcome the world!"

Do you comprehend what He meant by this now?

He had overcome the lower elements in Himself, had transcended the flesh while *in* the flesh, and had demonstrated to man what man, Himself, could and must do in order to free his spirit.

There is great unrest in the flesh of man today. The lower self is weary, sick unto death of the struggle. When the truth can be revealed to it, this lower self will gladly surrender to the higher and release its clinging to the flesh, and merge with the higher self so that the two, as one, may now enter into the higher dimensions to which they are long since heir.

I have revealed much this morning.

Evening

The very hairs of your head are numbered. Just so, there is a limitation known only to God, the Father, of the souls to be enfleshed on this planet Urantia during its existence in this outer universe. And places have already been prepared for them in the succeeding dimensions to which they are destined to progress.

There is a tide in the going and coming of souls here like the tide of the sea—a ceaseless flowing in and out as God breathes the breath of Life into new human creatures and withdraws it from countless others who have reached the moment known only to Him when they are ready for the change.

Each individualized soul is here to perform a service for the Father in expressing that infinitesimal part of Him, and many and incomprehensibly varied are the services beyond the understanding and grasp of average man.

Can you see any value in a sordid, wasted life? Yet its sad example may have shown others the path—while the misguided soul has stored up experiences from which it must later gain.

Each soul has a pre-existence in the House of the Father and is conditioned for entrance into Life here. *But each soul has the gift of free will from the beginning and the nature of its reactions to the "conditioning" determines its choice of and affiliation with the earth body into which it is born.*

By identifying itself with the physical outlet it chooses, through exercise of free will, it takes on materiality and God's spirit becomes an individualized soul. Many spirits deliberately choose residence in lowly evolved human bodies with the God urge to raise them to a higher spiritual level. But often the burden of the flesh proves too much and the newly evolving soul cannot overcome the trials of the flesh.

Its punishment is no less for *not* having overcome, but its reward is greater for *having* overcome, and it must be remembered that many spirits, for whom fine earth bodies have been prepared, have sacrificed their birthright on the altar of flesh.

It cannot be judged on the physical side of life what any indwelling spirit has accomplished or failed to accomplish in a first-life experience here. God, who is mindful of the sparrow's fall, is much more mindful of Man's. He is watching the free will unfoldment of His children with tender and loving compassion through His appointed servants. And no expression of God's is lost in the final ultimate.

This is a big and deep subject, difficult of explanation. I have only been able to touch your consciousness with it—and inadequately as yet.

•••

May I add this one thought more: I had planted it in your stream of consciousness and it reached the surface some moments ago only to slip back into the consciousness of your deeper self with whom I dwell.

Have you ever pondered upon the force that keeps an ant the size of an ant, a fly the size of a fly, and an elephant the size of an elephant? And why this force or intelligence never permits the elephant to be produced the size of an ant, or the ant the size of an elephant?

What do you suppose keeps a human or any living thing from growing out of all proportion to its environment? Know then, that everything in the universe has its appointed size and form in time and space.

Actually, if you were the size of an ant, you would possess no less intelligence; and were the ant the size of an elephant, it would possess no more intelligence.

But everything in God's universe occupies the time and space intended at any given moment for the function it is supposed to perform. The ant is in its place and you in yours. To the ant, the sand is the universe; to the sea, the sand is the endless bosom of God; to you, who see *beyond* the sand to the heavens above, new dimensions beckon beyond time and space and all things, big and small.

•••

Note: When this dictation had been completed, before this "postscript" was added, the *receiver*, on rereading, had the sudden feeling that a most important thought had been left out, a thought which contained the key to the entire message. *This thought*—as underlined—was then given, and anyone studying the contents will readily realize its vital significance. The withholding of this thought to the finish and then its insertion, with the message to be completed by it, is strongly evidential that the material was dictated by an intelligence, separate and apart, from the receiver.

October 21, 1941

You have remarked upon the miracle of every element fitting into every other element, of how all elements in the universe operate in interchangeable relationship with one another.

You have been close to the perception of God the Father, in action. The universe is His Being and all elements are the result of His limitless expression.

Something is always happening to every particle in the universe in accordance with the effect of other particles upon it. Gases are changing into solids and solids into gases under conditions of inconceivable heat and cold and an impasse in Nature's processes never occurs. There is always a point at which even the most resistant element can be fused with another to assume a new form in the blueprint of God's plan.

Changes are occurring in your own physical body which would astound you were you conscious of them. Elements which are serving you are wholly unconscious of this service as they serve conditions comprehensible only to them. You are dependent for existence in this material world upon an aggregation of elements organized by your entity to permit your manifestation here. When this entity releases its hold upon these elements, other forces instantly commence laying claim to them until your entire body, through what you call putrefaction and decay, is dematerialized, returning to dust.

Would any human, looking upon a pile of dust, ordinarily pause to consider that its elements might once have constituted a portion of a fleshly body? But air and water and other elements, too intricately related to mention, have also entered in, and have been drawn into other forms of expression in this universe of perpetual motion. God *moves* in a mysterious way His wonders to perform!

Ponder well and long upon the word "*moves.*" It contains great meaning. Nothing in the universe stands still, ever. Something is inexorably happening to everything at all times in all space. The planet Urantia is revolving and also traveling toward an unrevealed destination and a moment in earth time when its elements, too, will be released, broken up and transformed into new worlds, so that new expressions of the endless, untiring spirit of God may manifest.

Everything then, the infinitesimally small and the infinitely large, has a direct relationship to everything else, and there is a plane reachable by highly advanced intelligence, when communion may be had with the elements, a language beyond the faintest comprehension of man, with which high intelligences talk to the elements as Gods in their own right and maintain permitted dominion over certain planets and worlds as licensees from the Father.

When these high intelligences say, "Let there be light," then there *is* light, after the Word of the Father.

The elements respond to the animating voice of intelligence which sets them in motion, revolving in their own orbits of activity in accordance with their nature and form at that moment.

In like manner, you are learning to respond to the direction of Higher Intelligences and are gaining immeasurably thereby, for every element and entity in command of even the elements in the form through which it manifests, advances to higher states of Being and Expression *in* the Father only by *willing fusion* with the spirit of the Great Intelligence behind all things.

This is the plan of unfolding creation. More of this later.

• • •

Fear not. The whole Pacific area is to be shaken, including the islands of Japan, and nature's destruction will give men pause.

There will be a great tidal wave—greatest of modern times—the effects of which will be felt on many shores.

The era of great mental and physical changes on the planet Urantia is close at hand. You will see more and more signs of it as your own preparation is speeded.

Do each day what is given you to do and know that each day is of increasing importance, for it has been said that time and tide wait on no man.

You have witnessed the protection accorded you in your *Mark Twain* work. This is for a purpose beyond your own personal interest and effort as was revealed to you this morning, the way all elements fit together, one into the other, so do *events*.

Entities from many points on the planet Urantia are moving toward one another in service and will join as do the elements to provide a band of spiritual strength encircling the earth in the coming time of chaos.

You have foreseen this awesome period for which you and others like you have been prepared these many, many years.

Fear not. Much may fall around you, in the movement of *elements* and *events*, but you will prevail. Sleep well. You have an appointment tonight.

October 22, 1941

A door is shut that a bigger door may be opened.[1] The value of your contribution to the *Twain* picture *cannot* and *will not* be lost, but your value in other directions is even more, and you must be free to move on, for world changes are coming fast and your services are needed.

You will scarcely more than have left these vibrations where you now are than the new things awaiting you will be disclosed and the next steps made clearly apparent to you.

Certainly you have had evidence of forces working in your behalf which have resulted in your transfer to California. These same forces have been preparing to *travel* that way. Your preparation has been swift and the time foreshortened. Be not disturbed at surface happenings and know that nothing basically can affect you any longer or the fulfillment of your ultimate destiny. You have come too far and have been too well tested.

---

[1] On this day Harold received notification that his services at the studio were terminated.

Events will establish so firmly in the entertainment as well as the philosophic worlds as to make you a commanding figure, with the power to dictate in place of being dictated *to*. This day is not as distant as you may think.

Meanwhile rest secure in the knowledge and faith that all is well. If it were not so, I would have been permitted to tell you. Last night you conferred with intelligences during sleep concerning these future plans and developments of which you are not now conscious. This conference was in anticipation of today's happening at the studio.

I repeat—all is well.

October 23, 1941

Agrippina is here. She remembers you well from the days of Germanicus, for you were that ruler.

And, even today, you carry a link of the Germanicus personality in the sound of your name "ERMAN" which has a relation in vibration to the personality you are now expressing through your entity.

The names that humans bear are not as haphazard as they may seem and strike the note in *sound* of the entity's true vibration. The identity of the entity never changes; only the expression of the entity through succeeding earth bodies as it reacts to different external happenings and conditions.

As Germanicus, Agrippina wishes to recall to you that you were surrounded in the life of Rome by unspeakable intrigue and put under the cruelest of pressure by those associated with you who prostituted their government offices by abuse of power, betrayal of public trust, and lustful exercise of the flesh.

Agrippina herself was not immune to the sly and treacherous influences of men close in your confidence and failed you on several occasions when you were sore in need of her support.

That you were able to stand against the tide of evil all but engulfing you and hold high to a code of service was one of the miracles of those days. Tried as you were, you clung as best you could to principles which held back the hordes who would have completely debauched the weak and the defenseless. You were feared and respected, as well as hated—betrayed in this time by your own brother.

But today, in this life, you find yourself surrounded by many of the same misguided entities, now having gained power over the masses, not alone in government positions but as the heads of great entertainment enterprises, particularly the motion picture industry.

You have returned to earth to complete this "unfinished business," to atone for mistakes you made, more of the head than the heart; and Agrippina, who finally gave her life because of her association with you, is one of a band of entities marshalling forces in this next dimension to aid in the great world battle which is to come.

As Harold Sherman your rule over the consciousness of humanity is going to be far greater than that of Germanicus, for you are to use weapons of much finer and higher power, the kind of weapons that these misguided entities cannot successfully combat.

Your present personality is resisting this dictation somewhat and making it difficult for Agrippina to say through me what she wishes. But she sends greetings to Martha, once a sister of hers in the long ago. And she instructs me to say further: "Yes, Martha, you, more than I, have earned the right to serve with the entity now known as Harold Sherman, but we are closely grouped together karmically and will meet on future missions. Be not disturbed about your past. It will be revealed in good time. But you, too, as your inner feelings have told you, have come a long, long way. And your union with this entity is not alone of the flesh; it is of the spirit. Such a union is needed and was so designed to be, in order that you both might give to the other the strength required to meet the tests of your present and last earth mission.

This is all for tonight.

October 25, 1941

You have seen trees bent and misshapen by the prevailing winds. Gaunt and hardy they stand, oft rooted in barren or rocky soil, their trunks and limbs bowed before the tempest but unbroken and unyielding. They do persist in the face of all seeming earthly adversity.

And you have seen trees of the same seed, in other climes, amid the gentler breezes of less prevailing winds, rooted in kindlier soil and finely shaped; yet, with all the smilings of Nature, destroyed by the ravages of tent caterpillars.

Where then are the advantages of too protective influences? The one tree stands, physically not a thing of beauty, but braced and strong against the elements; the other tree is blighted amidst surroundings of peace and apparent security.

A life rooted in the spirit may continue to thrive in and under conditions that would not sustain the flesh alone, conditions millions of souls are going to have to face in the next few earth years.

The prevailing winds of fortune will blow exceeding hot and exceeding cold, over great stretches of the earth scorched dry by heat and drought or frozen by early frosts and unseasonal cold. This unbalance will be increasingly noticeable in the atmosphere as earth and all the elements related thereto react to the actions of man. And the bowels of the earth will gurgle with this same great restlessness, all elements reaching a stage of higher and higher agitation until a breaking point is arrived at when this planet and all upon it will feel the interchangeable ebb and flow of forces, wrongly used, seeking readjustment.

It is then that Higher Intelligences, working with those enlightened souls in the flesh, will exert the full power of their cooperation, in that cataclysmic time, to enable the stalwart trees rooted in spirit to withstand the "psychic blow." These "trees" have been planted on earth to provide a "wind break" for the "wilderness of human trees" which must be flattened as by a hurricane unless so protected.

You and the Tree Planter of old are among those who have been developed to meet the tempest of fleshly happenings. He has helped prepare the way for you and to nourish the soil in which you have been rooted. You will stand straight and strong against all the winds that blow as his tree falls, having served its time and place in the scheme of earthly things. But his spirit will rejoice for he has left a young, vigorous tree in his place, into whose roots he may still pour the nourishment of spirit.

This is a poor parable rather weakly dictated to try to convey a great truth of cosmic relationship.

You are a branch of the tree of everlasting life, individually rooted in the spirit of God, the Father. How you grow and how you eventually learn to withstand and then to gain mastery over the elements is up to you. But when your tree can be planted in barren soil and survive against the storms of human experience, you may know that the time is near when you may be permitted to stand alone.

The Tree Planter has watched over you carefully and is pleased. Let all prevailing winds blow; you may bend before them but you can never more be uprooted.

October 29, 1941

New conditions and opportunities are coming rapidly your way along the lines of your intended interests and activities as you will perceive by the first of the week.

The way has been prepared by others, serving consciously and unconsciously the purposes for which you came into this life.

As the Tree Planter has instructed you, "Watch how the pieces fit into the pattern."

Mark Twain was and is a stepping stone but it is only one brick in a building you are erecting which is destined to catch the attention of the entire world.

The building will be unlike anything seen on earth before, and your enmissioned brothers, who will join with you in the building will help you set up a spiritual shelter for the millions who will then be weary and heavy laden, not knowing where to turn, nor what to do, without hope and without faith.

Could any work be more needed or more inspiring? Reaching the souls of humanity is vastly more important than reaching their minds—or their pocketbooks. These have been pandered to by merchants, politicians and charlatans. But even the churches have failed to touch the human soul. This is to be your mission—you, in company with other brothers of earth and dimensions beyond. Your physical body is being strengthened for the work ahead; as well as mind and spirit. The plan is unfolding with accelerated speed to keep pace with the quickening tempo of world events.

Be not disturbed by surface happenings; they are no more to be regarded than debris on the surface of a mighty river whose current runs true and deep, unmindful of the passing scum.

You are a vital part in the stream of service which is flowing Godward and will carry a goodly portion of humanity with it.

October 31, 1941

If you could see the ball of earth with an X-ray eye, you would pass through layers of mineral, of gases, and of fiery heats down to a magnetic center. This center glows with the incandescence of an electric coil as the magnetic energy in the ether flows through it, sustaining the earth in its place in the heavens with respect to the other planets and suns. Imagine, if you can, the magnetic pull on all parties in the universe which holds them in their own relative position. Can you not sense vast intelligence behind this entire operation?

In much the same manner you are held in your own plane of existence until you are prepared to enter another through having raised the character of your own vibrations which then automatically releases you from a lower magnetic influence to a higher.

This is the normal method of progression but the invoking of lower and higher vibrations in the earth body has confused the forces, making this release one of great difficulty. In fact, with this mistake transgressing the laws of Being, it has been impossible for the imprisoned souls to separate themselves from the magnetic pull of the lower elements in them until Higher Intelligences interposed their own forces in adjudicating the ages-old complication.

You cannot respond to the magnetic pull of higher dimensions until you have reached that state of vibration within your own consciousness. Otherwise you will continue to attract to yourself only those things and experiences within the range of your limited capacities. This is the only *way* in which the Father could, in all justice and mercy, permit His Creation the exercise of free will in approaching Him. Nothing is withheld from the aspiring soul or any evolving part of God's creation the instant its reaction to external experience has qualified it for the next upward change.

Everything is revolving in an orbit of its own. There are tiny worlds, as you know, in the whirling atoms; there are universes in your own cell structures. And in and through all these manifestations is the presence of the Great Intelligence feeding His children with all the wisdom and love these parts of Him are developing the capacity to receive and express, at each given moment of their unfoldment.

Do you catch the vision of a great rhythmically swirling cosmos of inconceivably, incessantly interchanging elements to all of which you are in some indescribably wonderful manner definitely related? Yes, even to elements now existent on the most distant planets! The same Presence, in which you dwell, is there as here, and where it is, there are *you!*

But, because you are tied to this house of flesh, your comprehension of these things has been dulled. You think only in terms of time and place but there is a plane beyond wherein the magnetic pull of what you call time and place no longer exists. Then you are free to traverse great regions of the kingdom as a trusted servant of the Great Intelligence and incomprehensibly sweet will be the joys of such service. But this is taking you far, far ahead on the path of progress beyond your present stumbling feet.

Know, however, that you have raised your own vibrations much in the past year and are rising, as a consequence, above many conditions which can never more exert a pull upon you. You and Martha, through your understanding and development together, generate a power which protects you against many destructive forces whirling about you. This power will be more and more manifest to you as your development continues. And your own magnetic pull will attract many earnestly seeking souls, causing them to put their feet upon the same path, this, in itself, *increasing* your own power.

5
Hollywood
November 1941

November 4, 1941

There are two kinds of sleep.

One is the sleep *in* the body until the real awakening comes. The other is the sleep *of* the body each night, during which time the entity is often liberated for duties beyond its flesh house.

Since the soul, as the Tree Planter has said, possesses a body, it may lay it down, on occasion, as one does a coat, and step outside. Yet a thread-like connecting link is always maintained between flesh and spirit, something akin to the discharge of force between a broadcasting station and a receiving set.

There are two methods of projection—an extension of your consciousness to a certain point while still in the body, and a sending out of your astral self. In the first, your consciousness in the body is sustained and you are made aware of conditions and happenings at that outside point. In the second, your body consciousness is suspended and you are aware, through the astral, of happenings at the point of contact.

An entity, undeveloped in astral traveling, has difficulty in bringing back to the body and transferring to the body consciousness a clear record of its journey. Sometimes such a person will awaken with a vague, dreamlike recollection as though they have visited some distant place. But because the body has experienced no such visitation, there is nothing *associative* that can help the body consciousness *identify* the impression.

For this reason, many individuals deny or reject fleeting evidences of activities in the astral when returned to body consciousness.

Since the Spirit came from its place of "conditioning" and entered the body at birth, it has naturally a greater freedom of movement than the body. The Spirit entered in and took up its abode in the house of flesh and therefore is free to leave when the body itself has reached the end of its existence. If the spirit was of the earth earthy, it must also perish with the body, but this is not so.

Yet the long journey back to the Father must be made through *individualized conscious* existence. The journey is not one of time and distance, but of soul development. You are given as much as you can stand and as much as you have earned in the way of knowledge with each step of progress.

Your inner self is in touch with intelligences from higher realms, at times, and materially benefited thereby. This communion is dependent upon your degree of development. You are aided also by advanced souls on this side of life as your spirit reaches out for wisdom and understanding. Nothing is withheld from you that you are ready to receive, and as you gain greater command over the flesh house in which you reside, you may disengage yourself from its hold upon you, more and more, to your own deep spiritual advantage.

This "letting go" of the body is not a difficult or complicated procedure. In due time you will be shown the way.

November 5, 1941

Understanding comes from closeness to reality. A pig's snout is in the trough too much of the time for it to see that there is a world outside it. Many humans are pandering to their sense appetites so continuously as to be almost wholly blinded to the true forces moving in and about them.

A skunk surrounds himself with his own smell and drives all else away from him. We all have radiations dependent upon our interests in life and the nature of these radiations determines what happens to us. If the radiations are pleasing and harmonious, they are sensed by others who are drawn into our vibration and *good* results from such association; but if the radiations are displeasing and discordant, like the skunk's odor, others are repulsed and will have little or nothing to do with us.

There are odors to *actions* as well as odors to *things*. The olfactory sense exists also on the astral and spiritual plane. Music has an odor—a rare perfume, as changeable as the moods but which our poor physical senses cannot register. Your soul or entity can *feel* music as definitely as you can touch a beautiful flower with your fingertips.

Everything really merges into everything else at some stage of creation's processes, so that light can become sound, scent, and scent, color, and color, a corresponding degree of heat to the end that an entire symphony of creative expression is realized through the interplay of elements. But it requires the spirit, operating in and through these elements, to perceive these wonders and to band them together in new and countless forms.

You are now being given a glimpse of Reality in motion. Much of it escapes your senses. But one day your entity will posses a body instrument sufficiently refined to register the grand symphony of the universe and then your soul will know the unspeakable ecstasy reserved for those who have sought and have found harmony in the spiritual house of the Father.

November 6, 1941

Each day the band of service draws together with new entities appearing on the horizon, being readied for service. There will be no mistaking members of this band when they are brought in contact with you. It shall be your duty to awaken some but many are arousing from their long sleep in the flesh, having had vague, restless dreams and yearnings, and all they will need will be a tap on the shoulder and the right word to enlist them as fully prepared soldiers in this spiritual cause which means so very, very much to all troubled souls on this dark planet.

You are to receive what will seem to you amazing support. An organization will spring up under your direction as though it has been materialized with each entity, man or woman, in his appointed place, by talent, past preparatory experience and design. Many were the kinds of artisans required to build the temple made without hands, and just so will this temple of the living God—the Great Intelligence—be built. Its dome will shelter all humanity; its foundation will hold firm while the whole surface of the earth and all human forms upon it tremble in the balance between chaos and regeneration.

You have been told to watch the rapid acceleration of events. Again, we say: *watch!* You cannot be prepared too soon and you had to be free at this time to be about the Father's business. Take no thought of the morrow. Sufficient unto your needs is each day thereof—but great forces are at last to be released through you, and united with you.

For this reason the physical body has had to be improved in health. You have prayed for inspiration and guidance. It will be increasingly yours from this moment on. Thoughts and ideas and plans will commence flowing in, as a stream from your brothers in higher dimensions who count upon you as an indispensable proven link in the mission to which you have given so many years of your earth life in preparation—yes, and long before that!

Rejoice that the time is close at hand even though it means the assumption of *great responsibilities*. You will be given strength and the wisdom required to meet situations. The evidence you seek to support the stand you must take will be supplied as the occasions arise.

Fear not! As you watch and hold yourself in readiness to act, as impelled by the inner voice, you are being watched over.

November 9, 1941

Life, as the Tree Planter has said, is an "individual proposition." But one's sense of separation from another is felt more in the flesh due to the interposing of the lower self which has only to do with the earth body. True, these fleshly forms are dear to us and we can realize intimate association only through them, but this union is as nothing compared to the contact which can be made when the real entities can be freed from the physical.

In dimensions where to *think* of a loved one is to *be* with that loved one, if such desire is mutual, there is association beyond your comprehension of sex and far more stimulating, with the two entities embracing one another in an expression of ecstatic understanding and devotion.

It is really the minds or entities of two loved ones which vibrate in harmony on the earth plane and cause the glow of spirit to be fused throughout their flesh bodies in physical intercourse. Then, how much more so must be the attunement of two such souls when they meet in higher dimensions without the drosser insulation of the flesh!

No good thing is ever ultimately lost in nature. God's law of conservation is operating through all the changes of evolving forms, preserving that which is an advance upon the old.

As was emphasized in a previous communication, you are evolving upward through Time which exists in layers and stands still. You move through *it!*

Separation, then, when one soul leaves the physical body in what is called Death, is only seeming. The physical body is left in its layer of Time area and its elements eventually reabsorbed, to be re-embraced and used in new evolving forms; but your entity, so released, is now vibrating in a new time-area dimension.

Naturally the soul left behind, still inhabiting an earth body, suffers a sense of almost inconsolable loss for it is left with the dead shell of the earth body from whence the spirit has departed. There is no communicable evidence of continued existence here.

As long as the flesh body of the loved one was animated by the spirit in this time dimension you had contact with it. But all life expression is synchronized on different time levels, and to exist in a state beyond death, you cannot exist here.

How can I find words in your limited vocabulary to convey to you what happens in transition from one dimension to another?

Can I say it this way? If a soul could overcome the body concept of time in the flesh, it could bring earthly immortality to the body. There would instantly be established such an at-one-ness with the eternal power of the Father that the body elements would take on a timeless consciousness. *But* all progress for these elements would cease since development beyond their present form would be arrested in this timeless state,

Life expression through layers of Time means continual, eternal progression. Your individuality is preserved in the timelessness of the Father as it progresses through Time-Space dimensions.

You and Martha have been joined together in missions of service before. Have you been lost to each other? No—you are co-existent in the Father's universe and, while your entities have not always entered earth bodies in the same layer of Time dimension, you have never really been separated in spirit.

How can I make you see? The physical body is not the real you. It is subject to the time-consciousness of the time dimension you are now in on the earth plane. But your inner self has no consciousness of Time or Space, having its existence in the Father or Great Intelligence. And, since you and Martha and all evolving souls really have your existence in the Father, you are inseparable whether within or without a fleshly body.

Again let me try to get this comprehension across to you. The "I Am I," to you, is your only testimony of identity, but Martha's "I Am I" to her, is the same as *yours*. Do you recall an old axiom in geometry, "Things equal to the same thing are equal to each other"?

You are all a part of the same "I Am I" or God consciousness which pervades all universes, and you are, at the same time, as mysteriously wonderful as this may sound, conscious of and possessive of this at-one-ness in each other.

I wonder, will it require experience in the next dimension for you both to understand the glorious meaning of the "I Am"?

You feel now, each of you, so expressed, that one could not exist without the other. Each of you would gladly surrender his consciousness of "I Am I" for the other which means that you feel you would rather not continue to exist without the other. And yet, the very retention of this "I Am I" or consciousness of identity is necessary to your retaining each other!

But you are joined *now*, except as separated by your two physical bodies, as one Being.

No, you must not try to picture the countless billions of other souls on the basis of embodiment. This only serves to confuse as physical forms and concepts have always done.

You *know* that you exist but you cannot testify that anyone else exists. They *seem* to exist because of you in your relation to them but they can only testify that they exist in *themselves*. The "I Am I" in them, which animates all evolving forms of life does this.

You and Martha, expressing as you are, have been drawn together as inexorably as suns, like magnets, pull planets along in their wake. The law of attraction is no less operative between souls than it is between the constellations in the heavens.

It is all a part of the incomprehensible "I Am I" in expression. But this "I Am I" is all-pervading and your existence as an individualizing segment of the God consciousness insures forevermore the preservation of your identity in it.

So banish all earthly fears that physical separation or death can bring any loss of this identity to yourselves or to each other.

I have spoken long and with much stumbling amid a field of words, none of which could be picked to convey what is really meant.

November 23, 1941

The *time* for which you were born is close at hand. All the elements, circumstances, conditions and peoples necessary to the happenings and achievements in *that* time are gravitating toward a series of points which you call *present moments* when they cross the field of your consciousness in the flesh. But your Higher Self is already associated with these moments *now* and knows the pattern that you are supposed to fulfill on earth.

Events are occurring while you are apparently stalemated, which are going to be related to your destiny and will be recognizable to you later.

With your soul now awakened, you have but to follow your Inner Guidance to be led to the right action at the *right moment in time* to synchronize with these events.

Your destiny is far beyond participation on the screenplay of *Mark Twain,* as important as that may seem to you in *this* present condition; but a *coming* present condition will demonstrate to you how unimportant this activity is by comparison. And yet, those who would seek to take advantage of you will not do so, at the last, for you will then have come to mean so much in several public ways as to have commanded respect, with your name a desirable one with which to be associated.

Your Mark Twain play will open the biggest door for you, dramatically, and lead to the opening of many doors. This could not and would not have been written had you been still employed on the picture, Mark Twain. And for the sake of your own designed future, it is much more essential that you be established as an outstanding dramatist than one of a number of authors of a screenplay.

Developments will soon commence coming at an accelerated rate. You have needed this time to be gotten in better physical shape for the work ahead. You should have no concern over economic matters. Guidance now extends in this direction also.

The seeds you have planted and the ground you have tilled this long time on earth are soon going to give forth fruit and you will at last feel that you have come into the vineyard.

Watch, this next week, for the *first* of the *great* developments, which will mark the real turning point in your life expression and set your feet in the path toward accomplishments beyond your furthest fleshly dreams.

Be still and know that what I say is true.

November 25, 1941

The Tree Planter is nearing the time of his departure. He senses it and is torn inside. His astral visit to your apartment on Thanksgiving afternoon was only possible because of the lessened hold his physical has upon his spirit. The fact of this unconscious visitation has disturbed him greatly as a man might be disturbed on finding he had walked to the home of a friend in his sleep. But he was guided to your home by his desire and fondness for you in the care of his Thought Adjuster who helped him leave the message. Just now the Tree Planter senses the uprootings of a long and arduous past and suffers great travail of spirit.

Sympathy and understanding are needful to him, tactfully administered, for he asks nothing and seeks nothing and, in keeping with all developed souls, wishes to retire from the world and gather his spiritual cloak about him.

Christ preferred to prepare Himself and face his final ordeal of the flesh on earth alone. It is then that the Higher Forces come close and spiritual communion is established as a bridge for the departing soul to walk upon as the flesh grows weak and surrenders up the spirit which has animated it.

The parting with the body is not always easy for it clings to that which has given it Being and Intelligence with all the tenacity of its animal life. The elements in it sense the change that is coming when they, too, will be released, to take on new form and substance and respond to the command of new, directing entities and intelligences—just as the souls, leaving their physical houses, are brought under the jurisdiction and guidance of new guardian entities of the order morontia.

All is law and order in the universe as you well know. It is the law that you now dwell and render service in the flesh. You are constantly responding to orders from Higher Sources—and then comes the day when the final order is given.

The Tree Planter has heard this order coming from afar, and is resisting it only because the other half of him remains rooted in the flesh. But such an order will sound more loudly in consciousness as the summons quickens; and, one day, the Tree Planter will slip as quickly from his weary and worn flesh home as he did, momentarily, this last Thanksgiving Day, never to return.

Great will be his rejoicing then and, should he go on ahead, the other half of him will be sustained by him from the other side through a special dispensation, so that her path will be made easy and the way sweet beyond describing.

Fear not, nor be disturbed at heart. Great, cataclysmic changes, as you have repeatedly been told, are at hand; but you will know the steps to take as the occasions arise.

November 27, 1941

Do not be impatient. More is happening beneath the surface which is to have a bearing upon your future destiny and accomplishment than is now apparent. You are soon to enter a new phase—the most important one in your life, thus far—when greater power of expression is to be given you and when word of you and what you stand for will be spread to the winds, with seeds dropping in every community.

There will one day spring up many in divers places in whose consciousness has been planted your philosophy of life and whose demonstration of your teachings will inspire untold others.

The radio is to be perhaps your greatest instrument through which you will become one of the most widely discussed individuals of this present day and in tremendous personal demand.

Yes, that day is coming—and much nearer than you now realize. Have no fear of the morrow nor its demands. The resources you need will be provided, as will be the proper place for you to reside. Be happy where you are at present.

And watch events pile rapidly upon events as the world picture becomes more serious and confused. Nature's catastrophes will soon keep pace with those which man visits upon his fellow men, and the message you and those associated with you will have for the world will be imperatively needed.

All is well insofar as you and yours are concerned, so do what it comes to hand to do until your path is made clear. It will all fit into place in due time.

6

Hollywood
December 1941

December 1, 1941
The Tree Planter's service is ending and yours is just beginning. As his roots are loosened in the soil of earth yours are just taking hold. What he has helped plant, others will bring to fruit.

This may be done not quite as the Tree Planter has envisioned, for the younger roots closer to the changing elements in the soil of today and know better the chemicals of expression needed to beget wide public acceptance of the truth. But an aged Tree Planter protects what he has nourished, sometimes a bit blindly and too steadfastly and this is often the reason why those whose physical instruments are impaired through long earth service, are relieved gradually of their duties. They feel the burden of their accumulated years and the spirit yearns to be off.

And yet, long, faithful identification with a great earth responsibility leaves ties not easily severed either by soul or body. You have seen earth trees, knotted and gaunt, still clinging to life and putting forth meager leaves long after full usefulness is gone. And, sometimes, on closer examination, you see some tender shoots of this tree, struggling upward near the old roots, that need the protection of its sheltering trunk from the prevailing winds until they have become more sturdy and can stand alone against the tempests.

Through the years, these tender shoots have drawn strength, willingly given, from the roots of the old tree, and, finally, the old tree dies to make way for the new which, gaining power and sending its own roots down deep in the soil of life, needs to expand and cover the place once occupied by the old tree which would now, having served its time, only be an encumbrance rather than a help.

In somewhat the same manner are those souls in service, related to one another, with always the older nourishing the younger and then giving way that the younger, in turn, may be the *nourisher*, and so on in the unfoldment of time on the earth plane, like the rings of a tree, layer on layer, until the design of the Great Intelligence for this planet has been fulfilled by all entities heretofore, now or ever to be upon it.

This is why enlightened souls, looking ahead, may see their places in advanced layers of time as they are to unfold upon this earth plane. The physical or external expression of these layers of time has not yet come to pass but they are even now related to what has gone before and what is happening in every present instant.

Your roots are reaching down deeper all the time, drawing in forces in the form of new friends and acquaintances, conditions and opportunities all of which will manifest in greater and greater recognition of yourself as a personality with a message for humanity—and with the channels opened to present it.

In moments of change, there is always the wrench of separation and suffering and elements of uncertainty. But you have nothing to fear. Hold fast to that Inner Quiet and know that the breezes of true inspiration are blowing across the waters of your soul and immersing you in a sea of increasing wisdom and understanding. This you will need as the outer tides of world fear and hate go sweeping over the earth.

But you know now this one, safe retreat—the harbor *within* which protects you from all outer turmoil; it is here that you may be replenished daily to meet any earthly ordeal.

December 3, 1941

Your cup is soon to run over with good and important things. Long years have gone into the results which will now commence to show on the surface but which have been in formation all this period.

With each development will come increased responsibility necessitating greater and greater wisdom. The need for meditation as a means of inviting true and guiding inspiration will be more and more pressing as time and your opportunity *in* time *unfolds*.

But you will be led to the proper home for you where such meditation will be possible and you will recognize it at once when you have seen it. This home will be waiting and ready as all other events and things are ready to synchronize when your own movements are properly timed on the earth plane. Haste and impatience disturb or destroy developing vibrations which have to be reassembled and built up all over again, often many times, by well-meaning individuals who have not reached the proper stage of initiation. Countless humans are wrecking their own lives or disrupting their destinies by too precipitate attempts to speed a happening or an achievement.

It has taken you all this time to lay the groundwork, to gather about you friends, acquaintances, conditions and circumstances which are all now vibrating harmoniously, each contributing their part to the realization which is to be yours. And you had to be brought West by another project interwoven with your other interests and aspirations, in order to be at the right place at the right time.

Refer again to the message on the "weavers" and you will more clearly see the tapestry that your own destiny, which you have been pursuing so steadfastly against all obstacles—physical, mental and economic—has woven.

The world is soon to be drawn into this tapestry for the design includes world interest in what you are to do and your loom is to stretch across oceans, eventually, which weavers from many lands joining in to fit their tapestry with yours to the end that humanity may be served.

It has been pointed out to you that events are moving ever more swiftly, and you have been told of developments quickening in your own life. Is not the evidence appearing more and more each day in substantiation thereof? Seek to maintain an inner quiet and poise with respect to it all which will remain your greatest power.

I am as pleased as you, to be able to give renewed assurance that *your time* is near at hand.

December 7, 1941

Freedom of movement is going to be increasingly vital in the days to come. Your inner consciousness is already being made aware of certain developments with which you are to synchronize your physical movements. This accounts for your uncertainty of feeling in the matter of your being invited to speak to a Masonic order this coming Wednesday. Your inner self knew that your body presence would likely be demanded in another place in direct relation to the Father's business and caused you to decide against acceptance so that you would be free to move where you are meant to move.

Until one learns to follow Inner Guidance, his physical urges and movements constantly obstruct, retard and even destroy the Path intended of the Real Self.

The pattern of your life is being revealed more and more to you every day, and you are witnessing the *materialization* of new brothers in the flesh, who themselves have been prepared to serve with you *in* and *through* this unparalleled crisis which is approaching.

You have come this far alone, an initiation which is required of all who are destined to serve, since he who cannot stand alone can serve neither himself nor others.

But now you are to be joined, and *have been* joined by others, whose strength shall be added to yours. In this fraternity of souls there is no leaning, one upon the other. Each bears his burdens in his own developed way but shares his full spirit in harmonious and understanding cooperation so that a multiplication of God-power is applied to the task in hand.

Develop the mental habit of taking everything under advisement in the way of new proposals and invitations until you are able to consult with your Inner Self and make certain that the body is not involved in activities which might restrict the purposeful expression of your spirit.

There is no limitation in Spirit except as you dam its flow toward destined objectives by counter movements permitted your physical body through its desires and often well-intentioned but mistaken urges.

Can you sense the true relationship of your Higher Self to the lower animal self, and why it is so imperative that the *two* should be brought into completely fused harmony?

You are familiar with the old saying: "His right hand knoweth not what his left hand doeth." The right hand of God in man—his spirit—is often cut off from the left hand of man— his animal self, the human creature with whom his spirit has dwelled this long, long time.

Review now the message given you early in our communications—"The Right Hand of God"—and new illumination will come to you as to its meaning in relation to your present unfoldment.

Great forces are being readied to flow through you, and great inspiration. The only factor that can prevent the flow is the physical. Since your movements on the earth plane are limited by the physical, you cannot be where you are supposed to be at any specific point in time and space unless your control over the physical is such that it remains subservient always to the will of the Higher Self in you.

This thought has been stated in various ways this morning that you may not miss its significance. Those who render great world service have stepped up their vibrations so they are no longer tied by the flesh. Their physical movements always coincide with the movement of the Spirit in them.

Yes, I perceive that the full import of this truth has finally come through into your objective world plane, and that you will endeavor to be guided by this revelation in the future.

How little men yet know of the forces in them and how they are to be used! How wanton is their abuse and waste of these forces! How lamentable their *willed* imprisonment in the flesh when the right exercise of this will could free them, almost instantly, from the ages-old mire in which their spirits have been floundering.

Your own spirit has been sickened by the mire you have encountered in many others. This revulsion of feeling is always experienced by the sensitized entity on its way out of the same mire. But you, through what you, yourself, have undergone, in company with your brothers, are to be a Way-Shower.

Make then your body *fluidic* to the movements of your spirit to the end that your destined objectives may be *directly* reached without loss of time, energy or place.

December 9, 1941

A shocking revelation of America's unpreparedness and incompetence in military matters is soon to burst upon the country as a series of reversals occur in lightning hit-and-run attacks carried on by the Japanese along a continually shifting front at sea and strategic points on the West Coast.

A proud United States, blinded by her own mistaken sense of power through bigness, is going to be reeling and staggering beneath repeated blows in the early part of the conflict which will awaken her peoples to the softness of their resistance and lack of iron-willed discipline which must be summoned and placed behind every united effort in order to match and hold off the fanatical attacks of a Yellow nation ablaze with hatred for Americans and bent on fiendish destruction.

Sabotage attempts will soon flare in various parts of the country, with spectacular damage accomplished in some instances. A national leader, perhaps two, will go down at the hands of assassins or under most mysterious circumstances. A plane and a train crash will take others. This is full war now in all its ugliest, most brutal aspects.

And we are to learn through it, that the animal in man always destroys, never builds; man, destined by his own wrong thinking to pay an indescribable penalty, will realize, almost too late, the healing, saving power of the Spirit.

Your work is to be made more plain as the crisis increases. It should even now be clear to you that our repeated urging you to "watch" and our stating that not one minute should be lost in preparation, was advice worthy of following.

We said that "event would be piled upon event" and, as you write these lines, the tempo is accelerating until average humanity will be dazed by the pace.

Man is going to pay now for his lamentable lack in understanding and wisdom. Where all races in this experimental world might have lived together in peace, the age-old difference in their ideologies and temperaments is leading them to destroy each other.

There will come, finally, a fatigue point when the flesh will be weak, thus giving the spirit a chance to be strong.

At this moment you will be enabled to accomplish your greatest work. Be calm and inwardly collected, knowing that you and yours are being cared for. Beyond that you need not know except as your course is revealed to you daily.

December 11, 1941

It is difficult to keep the body quiet when great changes are getting ready to occur in the spirit. The habits of the body cause it to wish to be in motion however worthless or aimless the activities. Those who have not approached that quality of "inner stillness" often wear themselves out with useless ramblings to and fro, unable to control the nervous physical urgings of their undisciplined flesh bodies. All wise and advanced souls know that the physical must be subdued first before higher powers of mind and spirit can manifest.

You have had difficult periods of testings when you have been compelled to await the right time for designed action. Each time you have permitted your body urges to attempt to force a condition in the process of materializing, you have found yourself thrown out of synchronization and have suffered exceedingly thereby.

Since your life forces are linked so intertwineably with those of other prepared souls, the fusing of these forces is a delicate operation requiring movements in time and space.

You are physically present in California, for instance, at this very time, for a destined reason. You are being held in readiness for your proper response *to* and alliance *with* this development when all factors have reached their appointed place in time.

Should other things develop, however temporarily satisfying to you in the ordinary expression of your talents, you would again be thrown out of synchronization with your intended path of progression. And, at this stage of your unfoldment, such a thing *must not* be.

Do not be impatient. Neither let yourself give way to fear or worry. You will soon find yourself harnessed *to* and *with* forces which can accomplish much in world service.

You have come a long, long way to stand where you now stand. If you could see beyond your present threshold and follow the steps you are to take into what you look upon as your future, you would be amazed and appalled. This is why much must be withheld.

Suffice it to say that you will be equal to the responsibilities soon to be assumed—that strength of body and mind will be given, for you are not to be in this world service alone—no, not by some thousands of developed souls, awaiting their contact with you in many localities of what is to be a greatly troubled and anguished country.

There is coming toward you—in Time—the opportunity for service you have seen and sensed from afar.

I will be with you then, as now, and we will go forward together.

December 13, 1941

You are holding up well and things are developing as you wait. Time is not being lost as it seems on the surface.

You should get some gratifying news the first of the week which will bring you a step nearer the conclusion of plans in the direction in which your destiny lies.

Any other pursuit than the *right* one for you, however temporarily profitable, would be obstructive and this is why you feel inwardly upset when you try to find some manner of creative expression to fill this waiting period.

Your Inner Self knows what is ahead for you and is keeping the body subservient through a silencing of the fears and worries which have caused you to move wrongly in the past.

You will not lack in inspiration and creative expression when the foundation has been laid and the channels for service opened. And once your real life mission begins, you will have to husband your time and energies because the demands upon you will be great.

Already you can perceive how long these plans have been in the making as contacts you established years ago now suddenly commence to fit into the present design. A weaver leaves some strands untouched until a later time when he gathers them all together and weaves them in and around the new strands set in place, just as though you have sensed only part of the design and have woven only as far as you have known, you have even put in some wrong strands and gotten others wrongly placed because you have, at times, lost sight of the design. But your weaving operations are soon to be quickened as developments make the design more and more apparent on the physical plane. Then the false strands will either drop out or be plucked out until the pattern of service becomes a thing of beauty and strength. There can be no weak strands remaining for all will have been too thoroughly tested.

The ways of God are foolishness in the sight of men. It has required the development of inner vision for you to have perceived the design of the Great Intelligence and to take your place at the loom as one of the brother weavers. But your place is now become indispensable and there can be no turning back for your spirit, in qualifying, has demonstrated its dedication to the task.

As arduous as the duties to be performed, there will be a deep, sustaining joy in knowing, at last, that you are rubbing spiritual shoulders with those equally qualified, both fleshed and unfleshed, all serving the same high purposes to the end that the ages-old design may be realized.

When this is accomplished the weavers, themselves, will be liberated from the loom and wheel of time which has bound them to this earth planet, and will hear the voice of the Great Intelligence, at the moment of transition, speaking words of sweetest music to their spiritual ears, "Well done, thou good and Faithful Servant!"

Yes, when your long period of service is concluded, and you have been true to the mission you have accepted, the reward will be beyond the testimony and grasp of your physical senses.

December 18, 1941

You have been a witness to the rapid acceleration of events and the beginning evidence of Nature's joining with man in the production of catastrophe. These are all consequences of long-planted causes and more and more damaging effects will appear. Unhappily much must be destroyed before a lasting spiritual foundation may be built and this time, the destiny of human creatures has reached the crossroads.

This piling of enmity upon enmity between races and classes of peoples is reaping an unspeakably terrible harvest. Economic and physical exhaustion will finally bring this holocaust to a halt. And then, with humanity stripped of the power of money and machine which it has basely and fiendishly misused, it can be reached and influenced by a presentation of the Truth.

The rebuilding of this war-torn era will be a rebuilding essentially of spiritual values, a blasting out of existences of the shams and hypocrisies and hateful prejudices. These will be replaced by a knowledge of man and his intended destiny here which will give to a subdued and sobered humanity, in which the animal nature has run riot, a true understanding of self and the ability to intelligently cope with forces long sensed but rarely comprehended.

You have known inwardly of this mighty task which lay ahead of you in what you call "time," for many years. You, with a host of other enmissioned souls, have been moving toward this moment in preparation and you will soon find the Path under your feet.

You have learned much in the curbing of impatience, and yet this lesson is still hard. But think how much more difficult it would have been for you, imprisoned in the flesh, with its physical limitations, to have been able to see the end *completely* from the beginning and to have had to *wait* through all these years up to now for the things which you came to Earth to perform to reach this appointed time!

The wait would have been unbearable. You would have suffered an anguish of spirit which you could not have borne in the body. Many another soul has not been able to bear even the burdens permitted him or the little that has been revealed. Some have committed suicide, unable to face the intuitive sensing of responsibilities they would soon be called upon to face or assume. This is why preparation for profoundly important service must proceed slowly. "Many are called but few are chosen." How sadly true this is, and how regretfully spoken the utterance.

But "be of good cheer," for you have overcome much and a glorious though arduous highway stretches ahead, just now veiled from view by a few remaining mists.

Realize now that mass consciousness is one of fixed ideas. For this reason, for you to have been accepted by mass consciousness as an outstanding identity in any one field would have prevented and precluded your acceptance as the identity you are destined to represent in the world service you are to render.

You have some evidence of this in the long struggle you have made to free yourself of the limiting stigma of "juvenile writer." Your splendid service to youth, through your writings, almost caused the public to accept you on the basis of that service alone—and to reject you on the basis of any other—however great your effort to gain such recognition.

Your Inner Self has known your destiny. I, Ara, have known. And your failings to succeed in certain allied literary fields—when it has seemed to you that your talents deserved the acclaim given to others less worthy—has been a source of great distress to you.

But, be no longer troubled. Once recognition comes to you for the task you have come here to do, all these other things shall be added. For these "other things" to have been added *first* would have resulted in the *submergence* of your real identity and spiritual force in the eyes of the public who would have expected a *different* expression.

Do you begin to see now the wisdom which has permitted you wide experience and yet has withheld the cup of real success from your lips? Too deep a drink of it would have left little place for these other things which mean so much to you and so very much to the world.

An idea, once fixed in the mind of undeveloped, unthinking man, is difficult to dislodge. *You* are to become such an *idea*, representative of certain spiritual truths, but how could this have been possible had you *already* been planted as a *different type* of expression in man's mind?

I hope that this revelation has eased your natural apprehension and self-condemnation for what you have regarded as failures in your past. Relax. All is well.

Hollywood, December 20, 1941

Astounding things are going to occur within the next two weeks which will rock the world. More changes are going to occur, even in this short time, than you or anyone has thought possible. And the American people will be shocked into thorough realization of the grim conditions ahead which must be faced. Simultaneously there will be realized the imperative need of maintaining the emotional stability of all—developing a national state of mind which can withstand the blows upon it from happenings within and without your country

It is in this service that you are destined to play an important part as the first step in the mission you have reentered earth life to fulfill. Fortunately you, with Martha, have been impressed to place yourselves in a basically "footloose" position, and this readiness to move wherever duty calls will be most helpful and protective in the period fast approaching.

Your chafing at inactivity will soon be at an end. By the middle of January, mayhap even sooner, the path your feet are to trod will be in evidence. It will call for a utilization of those powers and abilities you have built up through these long years of trying and testing experience.

Your conscious mind wonders at the opening statement in this communication but no elucidation as to the specific nature of what is to come is permitted tonight. Remain calm in the knowledge it will find you and yours untouched but it will arouse mass consciousness in America as nothing has done heretofore, and serve to clarify the realization of what is to be required of each and every one to successfully meet this unparalleled world crisis. Event piling upon event—an ever-increasing tempo! Watch!

December 22, 1941

"No man knoweth the day nor the hour" and this will be increasingly apparent as men in high places are taken by violent or sudden death. They will have served their time for good or ill but their going will not much alter the tremendous forces which have been set in motion.

These forces will require a change in the consciousness of mass humanity to counteract. A stream is not shifted from its course except by a gradual filling in or sudden landslide. But with the present tempo of world movements all shiftings will be sudden and attended by great violence.

Because of this, look for world-reverberating happenings with nature and man contributing disturbances of major magnitude. All vibratory planes cannot be upset as they are without great upheavals.

For a time, pressure upon pressure from many points will cause an intensifying of the frenzy among peoples until their feelings go beyond fear and desire for the preservation of life at all costs.

When and wherever this moment arrives, there will be a desperate revolt—mass suicide if need be—but revolt, nevertheless. You on earth are about to enter the most fiendish and merciless stages of the war when losing powers will seek to take all down with them by an all-out effort which will tax every resource and defense, and blaze with a temporary fury of attack unparalleled in the long bloody history of this planet. For a time, too, it must seem as though the more evil of the opposing powers must triumph, for all are steeped in the guilt of wrong human conduct.

But much is happening that eye cannot see, nor ear hear which is to play the deciding role in this most critical of all earth dramas, and you, with an army of enmissioned souls, will appear on this earth's dark stage at the proper time and illumine it with a spiritual light which [illegible].

As yet, destruction must have its way, and America is not to be spared grave and severe lessons as a penalty for peoples' blind disregard of anything but a seeking after worldly things.

But, in this great country, whose peoples are freer than any other, shall be found the strength of spirit and body to meet the challenge of this savage dying order. And, out of this travail, in years to come will emerge souls dedicated at last to the high purposes for which this planet was originally designed.

When the foundation has been laid, your work will have been done, and you will then eagerly await your release from this flesh body that you may answer the call of a higher destiny with those you love and with whom you have been associated this long, long time.

Watch for further evidences of what has been pointed out to you—startling happenings and changes and cataclysmic events. They even now hang in the atmosphere, so close are they to your present earth moments. And know, as these things come to pass, that your hour of great and far-reaching service is near at hand.

Christmas Eve, 1941

For ages mankind has envisioned the birth of the Spirit from its chrysalis of flesh and this has been symbolized in the celebration of December 25 as Christmas, a time when the Spirit was born into the world and its release accomplished through such advanced souls as Buddha, Confucius, Zoroaster, Christ and many others.

In this manner, once established, this date in earth history became associated with the time of physical birth of spiritual leaders; in fact, it became inconceivable to the masses of different eras that any great soul should have entered the veil of flesh at any other moment. So has the story of the resurrection been carried along the tide of Time since one who conquers the flesh has conquered Death. Similarity we find that, far back in the early beginnings, existing now as little more than vague myths, is evidence of those great ones who were crucified and yet did live.

In the consciousness of many alive today, as in all epochs, is an intuitive awareness of their spiritual birthright, now lost for a time, in the flesh. Feeling incapable, in themselves, of transcending the flesh, they reach out toward those who are able to manifest such dominion. They seek a Saviour, someone who can show them the way, having lost that way themselves. And many pay homage to the Christ we celebrate, on Christmas Day as One whose spirit has risen *from* and *above* the house of flesh, an attainment each imprisoned soul yearns to achieve of and for itself.

This is the present goal of humanity, shackled and blinded by the flesh as it is. But few are yet able to attain since they have not yet come to recognize Life, as the Tree Planter has emphasized over and over, as an "individual proposition."

Christ was indeed a Way-Shower, perhaps the greatest of many. He possessed the power to put the feet of countless souls on the Path. But He still *could not* and *cannot* take the steps for any of those who would follow Him. Those steps must be taken by the individual else a birth of the spirit, the miracle of being "born again" cannot come to pass.

The tendency of mankind is to attempt to *fix* things and events in *Time* and give these things and events a *place* in Time. But we are actually commemorating a *state of consciousness* which we ordinarily only consciously strive to emulate once a year in what we call "the Christmas Spirit," when giving is considered more blessed than receiving. The advanced souls know this for an immortal truth and law, and live the Christmas Spirit constantly. We sense this spirit from afar and only fragmentarily, so that our expressions of it are crudely manifested.

To give unselfishly of one's own self in service is the one priceless gift beyond cost, and not too many have always been willing to give of their own substance at Christmastime or any other.

Conditions, today, however, are going to so strip most humans of their earth possessions as to leave then little if anything else to give *but* themselves, and when this time and occasion arrives you will see spiritual transformations occur and the Spirit exemplified by December 25 expanded into an ever-present state. Once humans have experienced the real, they will gain no lasting satisfaction returning to the false; and then, with the spirit in them awakened, it will be possible for enlightened souls to reach them with the messages they will, at that time, be prepared to hear.

The new year holds much of devastation and yet of promise.

December 26, 1941

Less than a week of the aforementioned two weeks has elapsed and already much has happened, much of which you are aware and much of which you are not, as yet.

The demonstration today is evidence that events cannot be hurried but occur in their good time. And, just so, will the *right* things always happen as you learn to follow inner guidance and make haste more *slowly* but with *certainty* to the end that things, as paradoxical as they may sound, can be accomplished more *swiftly!*

A development started at the right time and with the right influences about it, is pre-destined to success because it originates with the *spirit*. But developments, however praiseworthy, which impatience attempts to direct through flesh channels alone is subject to the ills and mistakes and conflicting forces of the outer world and may fall entirely or attain mediocre results at best.

It is difficult to "be still" and listen to the voice within when the voice of apparent economic need speaks to you from without. Then is when you are tempted most to overrule your "better judgment," the dictates of the inner self, and strive with physical and mental force to hurry the materialization of a project before its appointed time.

What is the appointed time for anything *desired* to happen? When the soul is prepared to receive it. And those of us who have known of the intended destiny of those in our charge have sought to aid them in their preparation so that they might be ready in their good time.

Desire for service according to one's talents, developed and tested through life experience, causes such a soul to make union with comrade souls of like aspirations and missions consciously or unconsciously.

One's destiny, in this case, becomes collective; and, if his spirit is properly attuned to the Higher Intelligences attracted to him, the synchronization of his earthly activities is worked out for him as he concentrates upon each task at hand, so that he finds himself where he should be and suitably engaged at each right moment of his mission's unfoldment.

Because of the importance of your own selected mission, much has been required of you and special attention has been given to your development as well as caution taken, insofar as are permissible, to lead you in the right direction at different critical moments of your life expression.

Looking back, you can see ample evidence of this direction now.

But more important than anything that has happened heretofore in your present life experience here, is the activity that you are soon to enter upon. Your effort has been put forth, the spiritual contacts have been made and you have only to command your body and its body mind to "be still" and remain inwardly receptive, ready to respond to each clear and unmistakable summons as it comes.

You will recognize then that things just as astounding will be happening to you in their way, as are happening in the world.

But you have been told repeatedly that event is piling upon event, and this quickened vibration is going to require a quickening of your own tempo as your time of service arrives.

Hold yourself in readiness to *act*, even as you maintain your attitude of watchful waiting. By Wednesday of next week, look back upon the changes which will already have come into your life and the promise of the future.

December 27, 1941

Indescribable, unspeakable, in the earth sense are the experiences awaiting millions now alive on your dark planet in the year 1942. Many of those who welcome this new year in with senseless hilarity will be welcoming their own approaching doom or devastation.

Your President comprehends the need for changing the vibration of this new year's advent by proclaiming the day as one of prayer for America's guidance and deliverance.

Truly, with all the faults and earthly sins of the free peoples on your little planet, the only hope for the new order and its early implantation in the consciousness of mankind depends upon the United States of America.

Its discovery and development by advanced souls, leading bands of followers several centuries ago, was in preparation for what is now coming to pass. And many of those now native in America or who have come to America from other harassed countries are here on a missioned purpose.

But little can be done in the midst of chaotic turmoil such as will prevail, beyond attempts to stabilize. Insofar as is humanly possible, the emotions of this remarkably heterogeneous civilization that now constitutes American citizenry, and the determining of those who are to be in the front ranks of the spiritual armies when all military forces have exhausted their usefulness.

Then the era of rehabilitation will begin and the spirit of man will be the first that will need resuscitation—indeed resurrection—for without this revival and rebirth of spirit with the consequent resurgence of faith, mankind will not possess the strength to rebuild itself physically, morally, mentally or spiritually.

From the viewpoint of those beyond and above your physical plane, the appalling events attracted to the planet Urantia by ages-old wrong practices of its human creatures would sicken any consciousness were it not for our wider perspective which indicates to us a promised land of spiritual revelation when and after animal forces have had their last earthly day.

You, who were in at the near beginning, are privileged, with many of your earth brothers of that day, to be enfleshed during the concluding chapters of this long earth experience, and to play a dominant part arrayed as you will be against the forces of evil who will attempt to sway the animal side of bewildered human creatures in the mass, but will find an organized spiritual power, for centuries *anticipatory* of this moment in earth time, ready to protect the souls of millions who will be released from imprisonment in the flesh through the knowledge to be revealed. Against this knowledge and the power made possible to these awakened souls through it, these evil forces can no longer stand. But this they do not know as yet, having always conquered in earth's sad debacles in past ages. Here, however, in this era of Urantia's history, the way, at last, divides. And you and your enmissioned brothers are to be the dividing of this way.

Watch for evidences of your Path of Service as it opens up to you, and know—as fear and despair sweep this land of the supposed free, engendered by the unthinkable horrors to come—that this was all to be, of necessity, that true spirituality might eventually come, as the animal in man is subdued for all time.

December 29, 1941

As the situation grows more black in the Pacific, the woeful state of unpreparedness of your country's naval and military forces will be driven home upon the American people and pressure brought upon representatives in Washington as never before. Laxity has been the rule in America all too long; that and moral and ethical degeneracy and millions are to be punished as a result.

Heavy earth disturbances are due to add to confusion and destruction in certain war sectors and the Coast itself will feel tremors within the next few days. This unsettled condition of nature and man is to prevail increasingly during this period; it cannot be otherwise as effects growing out of a multiplication of interrelating causes.

Your own destiny rises sharp and clear, through and beyond these upset times. It is for you to remain calm and composed in the face of happenings which will seem terrorizing to many.

But the way is being prepared for you to bring all your creative abilities and spiritual powers to bear upon the present world scene which will ultimately lead to representation on radio, stage and screen and the public speaking platform. If you will check back through our communications you will find that what *has been* and *is* being evidenced since, has for some time been indicated.

You need, as you consciously realize, a reputation commanding nation-wide respect in your field of expression and this reputation is coming to you faster than you may guess.

I have repeated that no time is now to be lost; and that much is happening which is to concern you, even these days when you think yourself to be idle.

Synchronization of event with the right individuals is a subtle performance which has to take place first on the mental plane. You have known inwardly the direction of your aspirations but have not known outwardly the means or circumstances through which to bring them into expression.

Much will have happened and much progress made along these lines, as previously stated, by Wednesday of this week.

Watch for the demonstration of higher forces at work in and through you!

7
Hollywood
January 1942

January 3, 1942

Basically, more was accomplished up to last Wednesday than you have yet had evidence, but more will unfold this week that is now upon you.

It is good that you and Martha are giving thought to the many threads with which your life and lives have been woven. It will aid you to see the pattern to come more clearly. A painter studies a landscape before him but seldom paints it as it actually is, putting into it something of himself and his interpretation and outlook. Just so will you both be able, viewing the pattern of your lives brought up to date, to crystallize the picture of things to come—things this pattern needs to fill it out—giving to it, *consciously* now, something of yourselves, as you have not so recognizably done in the past.

As you do this, new threads appear or become visible which are now tied up with your destiny but only the awakened or awakening souls can see and become conscious of this spiritual landscape before it is materialized by happenings.

Often it is too late, when the uninitiated soul discovers or becomes aware of the poor handiwork the "hands of his Being" have wrought. Many are the wrong threads which have to be broken, then, and plucked out altogether, as the awakening soul realizes how far he has wandered from the pattern he had set out to make of his life.

No entity is compelled to fill out the pattern but all entities gain immeasurably by so doing; and those who do not, ultimately come to regret neglected God-given opportunities for right self expression.

Your lives have become so blended that you weave, for the most part, as *one*—which was so intended. And yet, few there are who remain true to the *destiny* which has called them together, so you should give thanks to those who, through the years, have been the threads *upon* which and *through* which you have been enabled to string the *pearls* of your own life accomplishments.

How wondrous is life and its meaning when you have begun to touch its true reality and purpose. There will soon come to you deeper understanding and enlightenment as you keep your spirits attuned to one another and the goal as it unfolds as a beacon light ahead of you, beckoning you on to more and more developing experiences, until, one day, in the full maturity of your expression, you both will have become a unit of service to the world, linked with other brothers and providing a spiritual battery of great power upon which millions may draw for guidance and strength.

Much is to be revealed to you both in the very near future. Fear not—even as disturbing things happen in the world about you, for this is a time of turmoil—but your time of *activity* is near at hand. We will go forward together.

January 7, 1942

Your waiting period will soon be at an end and when your producer leaves here it will be with the fixed plan to open [the new play] *Mark Twain* in Chicago. You may observe now how carefully events are planned that human mistakes may be guarded against and that the *way* may be sufficiently pointed to guide those enmissioned ones to the right place at the right time. The presence of members of the Stone family[1] in Chicago whose destiny causes them to be residing there at this time; the desire of Fred Stone to play on the road rather than in New York and to be with his family; the belief of Mr. Bryden[2] that *Mark Twain* belongs to America and should play outside New York, probably *Chicago*; the interest of the Occidental Life in you and the suggested plan of your broadcasting from *Chicago*; the desire you have to dramatize the life of Jane Addams, necessitating contact and association with Hull House, *Chicago*—all these factors actual forces crystallizing a power pulling you to *Chicago* for a joining with the group that your active service in this long prepared project may begin!

Things are happening as fast as it is humanly possible for them to develop on the earth plane, and the last link in the chain of forces taking you to Chicago will be forged by Occidental in the near future.

You are already prepared inwardly through conferences you have had with Higher Intelligences during sleep for the steps you will take when the arrangements are completed and the whole way lies before you. You will *know* at that time exactly what to do, how to act and what to say. Your leadership of men is then to begin. You will be required to serve first as a teacher and organizer and then as an exponent of these spiritual truths. But, while you are teaching others, you yourself will be undergoing instruction, through association with the

---

[1] Actor Fred Stone and his family, all performers, had become friends of the Shermans, who believed Stone would be perfect for the role of Mark Twain.

[2] Eugene S. Bryden, Broadway director and producer, was working with Harold to sell his *Mark Twain* play.

group in *Chicago* and through Higher Sources. A more active phase of service for Martha will then manifest itself and she will come into a clearer understanding of her vital relationship to this great mission commanding the services of so many fleshed and unfleshed brothers.

You are both going to be tremendously but happily busy with your life service expanded upon an unbelievably wider screen. The wisdom of your being held back in careful preparation this long time until world conditions were ripe for action will be more and more demonstrated. You have observed how you can talk to certain individuals now to whom you could not have broached these subjects a few years before. This is true of not only a few, but of millions. You even have the willing, and to an adequate degree, the understanding cooperation of your daughters in your movements, which should indicate to you that they, too, are being prepared. There are many intelligences associated with the many different phases of this same great project and the coordination of the whole is a task beyond your present comprehension.

You can only be a witness to what is happening with respect to your own relationship but be assured that similar synchronizing and coordinating actions are occurring throughout all manifestations of the plan on earth.

For, remember, these souls now engaged enfleshed themselves conscious of the mission each had volunteered to perform and each is now striving to find this design and weave his or her part of the pattern in earthly expression.

Some have become temporarily or completely lost in the flesh but others have taken over their threads of service and added to their own so that not one thread will be lost in the final weaving.

Could you presume any spiritual enterprise of this magnitude and forthcoming importance to humanity to be any less lovingly guarded, protected and supervised? Each day, from henceforth, watch for progress.

January 11, 1942

This week will find you far along on the way which is being opened up, in accordance with your vision of book, play and radio. You are now sufficiently awakened to perceive what you should and should not do with respect to your movements in any direction—when and when not to move—all of which will be of increasing importance in time to come. You have been tested in little things to determine your ability to respond to guidance before the period arrives when decisions will have to be made, on the moment, involving great responsibilities. Fortunately, life is so ordered that we may be prepared in "little things" first, in order that we may be given opportunity to react from the "inner self," employing our inner wisdom before major crises are to be met.

How few there are who see the true significance in "little things," but everything in this great universe is important and of first magnitude or it would and could not exist. Most humans yet do not possess the comprehension to see what the endless variety of little things and their reaction to these happenings have contributed to their present strength and weaknesses.

Think of the many things you have to do over and over and over again in your waiting experience—the literally *millions* of lines of dialogue you have written up to now, crude at first and immature but gradually attaining greater polish until today, you are approaching, through the *doing* and *redoing* of "little things," a power of expression which you have needed before you could make of yourself an instrument and channel qualified to bring through to this sorry world the great truths and revelations which duty is a part of your destiny.

Everything that happens or *does not* happen to you is *important*, and you must so regard it.

"Little things," whether they be domestic, routine, humdrum or not, seemingly—what developers of soul they can be! God is speaking to you constantly in and through "little things" and, one day, your surmounting of the "little things" by *right* reaction to them will find you on the height of attainment. Consider then your debt to these "little things," which seemed to you, at the time, so disturbing and irritating and inconsequential.

Your eagerness to do "big things" and to be associated with "big things" is understandable, but do you not see now that "big things" are only a multiplication in intensified form of a myriad number of "accomplished little things" which have been "put behind you"—forever in your service because you have mastered them, and all things given you of God are to be mastered and placed in your service

Oh, now—can you not begin to see the glorious destiny and promise which lies before you? All the elements are intended for the service of evolving man as he learns to attune his mind to them and command their servitude. Yes, the elements actually *sing* as they respond to *developed* Man's bidding just as they now moan, with a great rending of spirit, as they are compelled to wield their forces destructively at the direction of man's wrong thinking. You have heard the shriek of car brakes, the sound of elements crying out at this abuse—does this bring comprehension in a crude illustrative way? Everything in the universe is God or the Great Intelligence in expression and everything is interacting on everything else.

Any discord felt in a human's mind or body is the signal that he or she is interacting wrongly with something. Does this tell you something? Does it bring you any closer in understanding with the very elements which combine in conditions, circumstances and peoples to provide the little and big things of life?

You launch your dreams, your aspirations, your prayers upon the sea of these elements—the invisible carpet leading up to God's footstool, a well-worn but ever-new carpet upon which the feet of every traveler in every age has had to tread, a long weary road if the elements are not made to vibrate in friendly harmony with you. But your illumined spirit, awakened from within at your God center, knows how to command the seas and the tempests of Life—or the *elements*—in and about you! All developed souls have attained such command and know how to speak to the *animate* and *inanimate* in a language all *things* can understand.

Ponder well on this revelation. It is of first importance but I have had great difficulty finding words in your consciousness to convey it.

January 12, 1942

Space is the distance between an idea and its execution. Time is the medium which closes this space. Everything is happening in Space-Time as the outward manifestation of the spaceless and timeless Great Intelligence, or God. There is no space nor time to a thought or an idea in mind but it requires space and time as its media of expression. Each idea carries with it its own measurement in time and space in direct accordance to its nature and character.

A revolutionary idea—revolutionary in the sense of its potentiality to bring about *world change*—requires at the moment of its creation and expellation into outward manifestation perhaps centuries of time in spacial extension.

All humans then alive in this Time-Space dimension are destined to be influenced by this unfolding idea at the point of their contact with it.

Take, for example, a crude illustration, the idea of the first automobile. Peoples then alive were influenced by association with and use of the first cars; by so much their life habits and activities were changed. But many of these people were not influenced for long since they fulfilled their destiny and passed on.

But, just as they were influenced by the materialized idea of the automobile, they were, at the same time, being influenced by myriad other materialized ideas. And their reactions were having a bearing upon the character of their life expressions.

Now the descendents of these peoples have contacted the unfolding idea of the automobile at a different stage of its unfoldment, and all unfoldments, in compliance with universal law, continue with ever-increasing tempo so that the evolution of these later peoples is speeded up in direct ratio in the same moment of Space-Time.

Ideas are released to and through the consciousness of evolving humans as they have increased their capacity to receive. It then becomes their responsibility to adapt themselves to the impact of these ideas, once materialized, upon their physical selves.

Ideas come from the spaceless-timeless creative center of consciousness and enter the Space-Time universe of expression as do all evolving forms of life.

The externalized forms of an idea may die or pass away, but the idea, once created, continues to exist, and may be recaptured and launched again upon the sea of expression, often joined with another of its kind so that a new offspring results.

Thus ideas have their evolutionary cycles as do human creatures, for the law of upward progression is working through all forces in this ever changing Space-Time universe.

More of this concept at another time which is what the Einsteins of the world have been trying to grasp mathematically under the heading of relativity—the interplay of all elements one upon the other. It's a mighty and profound subject.

January 17, 1942

All is well. In another week your speech will be much improved. You will then be laying definite plans for the trip to Chicago several weeks hence. Consider now all that has been accomplished in every way—personally and otherwise—as concerns the whole family and your destiny in the comparatively short time you have been West. Has there been an equally progressive period in the entire little history of your earth experience here, this time?

Indeed there has not, but this progression will not *touch* the onward moving forces now working through and around you in the months and years to come when you find yourself a *personality* and *identity* to reach the consciousness of millions!

How can you longer doubt that this will come to pass as you are confronted with the piling up evidences of the carefully prepared steps you have been led to take?

You are, from this point on, to have spiritual allies in the flesh—men and women who will stand shoulder to shoulder with you in the great mission you are to perform with them. And you will be serving under a protective influence which will see you miraculously preserved, at times. You are to entertain no fears, physical or mental. Your training up to this moment has been intended to put you beyond such common human weakness.

What you will be called upon to do and say will require courage and steadfastness but your acts will be so synchronized with the times and conditions as to beget immediate and tremendous support from the many as a defense and a bulwark against the powerful few who will strive to oppose.

You will, in these critical times, have developed such a personal following that their confidence in you cannot be shaken and your leadership of them will be regarded as a necessary influence even by those who would like to defeat the high spiritual purposes of your associates and yourself.

This is not a happenstance universe, and mankind, running helter-skelter about in riotous animal lust upon this earth, is to have this truth driven into consciousness with drastic and impelling force.

Recognition of a Divine Power—a Great Intelligence—must and will come as the only means of liberation in the flesh.

Dire calamities lie ahead but the great awakening can only come through them.

But you will maintain peace and quiet within at all times—and know that all is well.

January 21, 1942

It is being made more and more abundantly clear to you that *guidance* is necessary in a world of conflicting and disordered forces.

You cannot always divine the *motives* of individuals who may approach you for favors or with proffers of seeming unselfish cooperation and, as your own position in life assumes greater and greater importance, any mistakes of judgment or decision bring with them more severe consequences and possible damaging setbacks along the path your feet are now traversing.

On the human plane alone everyone is subject to the influence of others, at times, either for their own good or ill, dependent upon the nature of the circumstances. But with the tempo of your specially designed activities rapidly increasing in order to synchronize with coming events, you must be able to move unerringly in matters of choice and determination.

Thus the particular value, among other values beyond price, of learning to respond to the Inner Voice and retiring to the Inner Temple of your own soul, that you may see again and again, each time more distinctly the pattern you are to fulfill in outward spiritual expression.

By envisioning the pattern or design you are thus enabled to fit the worldly pieces of time and space and peoples and conditions into it; but, without recourse to this plan, you are like a builder striving to erect a building from vague and uncertain memory rather than reliance on a blueprint.

Many there are who come into this life with missions of high intent and promise and who have become confused and enamored in the flesh. These persons still possess the "urge" to do fine things but they have lost contact with the pattern or "plan of operation" which they have brought with them. Occasionally, spasmodically, they catch a "glimpse" and then they are radiantly happy for a time as they throw themselves wholeheartedly into an enterprise. But they are soon "lost again" for they have not developed the capacity to hold communion with their true inner self and succumb once more to the demands of the flesh or worldly influences.

Bewildering and diffuse are the pitfalls on the highway to real spiritual expression and accomplishment on earth. And greater and greater has become the need as countless numbers of well-intentioned souls have failed.

The Tree Planter is right in emphasizing the anciently expressed truth "many are called but few are chosen." Yet you have the evidence that abundant opportunities for spiritual expression and advance surround every soul, as they have you, all through life, could each soul only perceive.

Learning to respond to guidance is the wisdom which must be acquired by all who would have protection while serving, and such protection all souls must have who essay important missions in this most critical of periods in world history.

January 21, 1942

Power is transmitted "on earth as it is in Heaven" only by direction of Intelligence.

When God *said*, "Let there be light" and then there *was* light, a great law is revealed, for to speak understandably and believably is to *beget!*

What is it that speaks? Not the voice which is only the outward manifestation of speech, but the Intelligence giving physical expression to itself. To speak thus is to command the ideas uttered to take form after their nature and kind.

To speak hatred, for example, is to beget hatred. Witness all the hideous forms which hatred has created in the world today!

Jesus spoke, and took great care in what He spoke, lest the "children of his mind" should rebuke Him who created them.

To *think* is to create in whatsoever *degree* and character of the thought expressed. Great is the confusion and many the bastard forms in most minds, creating for themselves through fears and worries and unwise desires surrounding conditions and shapes of things to come, unhappy and awful to contemplate.

For to all human creatures, high and low, has been imparted this God-power. This is the only power there is, but any individual's call upon it is in direct accordance with his developed capacity to utilize it with wisdom and understanding.

Mistaken use of this power brings about great world calamities when whole masses of humans so exercise it. And yet, so potent a force for good is this power that right use of it by even one enlightened soul can transform the world.

No limitation is placed upon any human creature but the limitation he places upon himself. When Jesus *said*, "I have overcome the world," He meant that He had risen above the misuses of the God-power by those opposed to Him through attainment of the consciousness that "I and my Father am one."

When this consciousness comes, one speaks with final and complete authority and steps beyond human error.

January 23, 1942

Action is soon to be your "watchword."

Action that will see you busy on a number of important "fronts" at the same time but all having an associative relationship. Now that your eyes have been opened you will witness a dovetailing of events and come to *await* their uniting as definite workings of a plan which has been bringing pieces of the pattern together—yes, from far portions of the earth—that this great world mission might be accomplished.

Individuals, possessing certain abilities and enlightenment, are inexorably swinging into line, seemingly materializing overnight to take their places in the almost miraculous "scheme of things." You are to have an army of spiritually prepared brothers at your command, and you *do* have now, as is evidenced by the extraordinary and unparalleled help you have received in making certain destined connections leading toward the achievement of necessary objectives as a foundation for the carrying out of your mission.

But you can have no conception, as yet, of the vastly greater army that awaits, ready to join forces with you when the "Zero hour" for the undertaking and performing of this mission is at hand.

Do you think for one moment that such a long-designed and carefully prepared spiritual program conceived for the benefit and uplift of mankind would be left unprotected and unsupported as the hour approaches for its launching?

"Seek ye first the Kingdom of God and all else will be added unto you." As you have shown yourself more and more worthy, more and more power has been given, and this process of development is continuing and *will* continue!

You are entering an epoch in your life when your worth will suddenly be recognized by many peoples; you will be much sought after for many much needed services.

Discrimination, based upon inner wisdom and guidance, will be increasingly required during these times. Many there will be who will try to justify and strengthen their own weak or false position through contact with you. These will seek to win your approval, if not directly, by inference. Your stand will need to be at all times tactful but firm, for the good will of all is desirable, since many can be turned from their present unstable and insecure ways, not by condemnation, but by quiet, unswerving example.

You no longer *need* what others in supposed advantageous commercial or other influential positions might "give" in exchange for some service or association with you which might prove odious or embarrassing or entangling. This period of "seeking" right conditions and peoples as means to a desired end is over for you.

You possess now the power, the development and the attunement with Higher Intelligences necessary to attract "your own" to you without confusion and with the minimum of error in choice. Your ability to recognize those who "belong" in your army of "spiritual compatriots" has now been sensitized and you will "feel" the approach of entities who are coming toward you in time and at previously designated places to play their part with you.

For instance, there, is awaiting you in Chicago, *fully prepared* for this moment—as there *will be* in *every* community you touch from this point on—a band of men and women who will *unite* in the furtherance of your *mission*. You have already been serving with many of them during hours of so-called sleep; you have known many far beyond this little present life; and you will sense this bondage when you meet them again in the flesh—just as Mr. Jenkins of Occidental Life sensed and so expressed his "bondage" with *you*!

Does the vastness of this enterprise as well as its importance begin to dawn on you? And do you wonder that the Tree Planter, seeing more distinctly the long road which has been traversed and the many pitfalls thereon into which many enmissioned souls have fallen, has his moments of doubt and concern assail him lest you not be true to the highest of the possibilities within you?

The oil of wisdom is being placed in your lamp. You are about to light the wick of understanding, and this illumination will show you the way ahead, taking your footsteps safely through the shadows.

You must not falter and you *will not*. Call upon me at any time and all times as you have so often in our long past. I rejoice that you have "awakened in the flesh" once more and that you are commencing to recall and recollect again WHO and what you are. This should add great power to you. Remember now how you took the "torch of service" from Joshua Ben Joseph and pledged yourself to carry His message down through the ages to the day now dawning? It has been a glorious—but oh, such an arduous—pathway! Yet, take heart, for the final fruits are to be worthy of it all.

• • •

Evening

Nothing can prevent your being where you should be at the right time. If you will check back over the factors that *had* to be present in California during this particular period of your residence which were not existent here during any previous period, you will see how exactly events have been fitted into one another. While, as the Tree Planter says, "mistakes and accidents occur," the pieces are fitted together just the same, in due course of time, and the plan moves forward toward its fruition.

Parts of the plan are arriving at fruition as certain developments take place. They are happening on such a wide front that many enmissioned souls cannot, at times, see or comprehend the progress being made.

There are still some important experiences awaiting you here which will manifest themselves this coming week. Everything basically is working out as it should. Apply yourself then to what comes to hand and mind and heart to do for the time is short, as has been said, when real activity sets in!

January 26, 1942

What is supposed to be yours can no longer be taken from you so rest secure in this faith. Great ideas and opportunities are swirling about you which, when their turn arrives for development and expression, can have a profound influence upon humanity. Your own position is growing stronger and more secure daily. While you seemingly are passing the time in waiting you have been undergoing a final preparatory period before one of the *great action phases* of your life, and when the "change" comes it will be swift and unerring. No more unsettled, uncertain conditions but direct paths of progress, all converging upon and contributing to the same spiritual goal!

Powerful forces are at work bringing the right elements and conditions around you and when these connections are finally made they will stay with you, many of them until the completion of your mission on earth.

So rest assured, as you have been, that all is basically well; and watch these events crystallize, drawing your services and talents into them!

January 30, 1942

Control and direction of the movements of a man would be simple if the operations were confined to one dimension.

But man is a complex organism, acted upon at all times by a multiplicity of forces within and without himself, only a few of which he really understands and many of which he is only remotely conscious of or does not recognize at all.

Under these conditions, it cannot ordinarily be predicted what any man will do in a given situation at any specific moment in time. True, each individual is coming under different influences every waking moment which he is attracting to himself but what he will do as a result of these influences, how much or how little—if anything—is determined by his past developed inclinations, abilities and experiences.

The higher developed the soul, the higher the influences in the way of Higher Intelligences attracted, and the greater the inspiration. This fact is self evident.

But this is all by way of trying to give you some comprehension of the colossal task undertaken by those in higher dimensions who attempt to aid those enlightened ones on earth in the performance of their duties.

To achieve earth results, one must work through and with many humans in all states of development who occupy positions of power or advantage. Oftentimes a man's secretary, however seemingly unimportant, may be the one through whom he, himself, may be reached and impressed to execute a certain service.

But a synchronization of the movements of many individuals in many different places that they all, unconscious of each other, may be led to be co-operative of their own free will and volition toward the accomplishment of a great goal, is a task of the first magnitude.

Often many forces, set in motion in the minds of key people, become sidetracked because of other forces in these people's lives moving in opposite directions. When this happens, the "planting process" must be undertaken painstakingly, all over again and new channels found, if the original ones cannot be reopened, that the "objective" may be reached regardless of possible multiple failures in the human equation.

This being so, it becomes understandable why a highly developed soul's fall from grace and consequent sacrifice of high spiritual promise and enmissioned responsibility is regarded as such a major catastrophe.

Consider how those interested in the work of Joshua Ben Joseph must have trembled as they, powerless to be of further aid, could only look on from higher dimensions, and watch Him meet the crises in the flesh as any ordinary man prayerfully hoping that He, tried as He was, might maintain the spiritual strength to surmount all forces set against Him.

Just so, has soul after soul been tried of those who have returned to earth these many times on missions of service to their unenlightened but desperately seeking fellow humans.

Each time the hold of the new flesh body is strong, and must be overcome. Few there are in each generation who can balance physical, mental and spiritual planes of Being. And yet, this must be done before they can become true and dependable instruments of service.

But, because you are required to work with so many who are not enlightened, you must develop sufficient force of *character, reputation* and pleasing, tactful qualities of *personality* as to be able to influence them, to cause them to desire to help you, often not knowing why or for what purpose, but enabling you to achieve the spiritual goal you seek through them.

You are a witness to miracle after miracle occurring in human relationships and responses—the present progressive dovetailing of enterprises which can be associated to great advantage in a later period of future time.

That this dovetailing has required even years in the various threads which have had to be tied together, does not now seem surprising as you commence to comprehend the forces which are at work and have been at work *with* you and *through* you and *around* you this long, long period which stretches back into a past you can not as yet recall, except dimly and fragmentarily, if at all.

Then is it any wonder that a week longer here or a month there is necessary, at times, to bring everything into focus at one point, making allowance for a failure of certain forces or influences to become operative in and through certain designed individuals at the moment desired since no soul is compelled to act in any given direction at any time except as the soul itself is so animated to do by its own choice and consent!

Patience, then, is a prime necessity on the earth plane as in our dimension. Perhaps there is no schooling so severe as the lesson to be learned in the acquiring of patience. And, closely linked with patience—welded together as the great trinity—should be faith and understanding.

Through understanding you realize why patience must be exercised and faith tells you that, with understanding and patience, the ways of God, the Great Intelligence, are accomplished on earth!

I have said much this day. *Watch*—with understanding and patience and faith—and you will see greater and greater miracles unfold before you, disclosing as they do, your Pathway.

February 10, 1942

The shocking state of America's unpreparedness and incompetence in high places is soon to strike the consciousness of the American people in full force. Woeful inadequacy and inexperience due to long years of self-interest, soft living and a false sense of security is soon to take its toll. Much confusion and hysteria is bound to result in the early stages of this fight to preserve the measure of freedom humans have gained on this dark planet after centuries of racial hatreds, greeds, jealousies and self-seeking individual and national ambitions.

Up to this moment, all races have missed the intended purpose of their association on this earth. There has been no true blending of racial qualities for the good of all, no sincere and genuine attempt to understand each other and to serve helpfully together. The higher races, in point of dominance, have done little to contribute to the betterment of the downtrodden, and now, as a self-imposed penalty, all races must be brought to their knees—economically and morally—reaching such a condition of physical, mental and spiritual exhaustion as to have wiped the slate clean of selfish desires and prepared the way, quite unknowingly, for the receiving of knowledge and inspiration from Higher Sources which could not have reached human consciousness otherwise.

You have been purposely led to witness the *drugging* of human consciousness by speakers and leaders, exponents of different isms or cults or social theories whose well-intentioned but ill-founded ideologies have blinded them to reality and the fact they are living essentially in a physical plane of life where animal forces, uncontrolled, still and will always run riot.

Spiritual powers, in the flesh, cannot cope with organized, diabolical physical force and mechanical might, except as it can counter with *greater* similar force and might, particularly since the guilt of human greed and man's inhumanity to man falls on friend and foe alike.

Spiritual power can only make its presence felt in a world aflame with animal passion and bestiality by attaining a *dominant* position through *physical* power, *rightly* directed, and then setting such an example of spiritual expression and conduct as to awaken spiritual perception in the consciousness of so-called conquered and conqueror.

It should be apparent that a nation and race, largely devoid of spiritual ideals or developed power of expression—if occupying the position of conqueror—will endeavor to impose its unspiritual mode of thinking and acting on all other peoples.

This has happened in past eras of history when the spiritual advancement of human creatures has been set back, and you are witnessing a repetition now on the widest and most fiendish scale of all time. But, a fundamental difference prevails of which the average human is not yet aware.

Higher developed souls, enfleshed and unfleshed, are organized as never before to help human creatures meet this crisis. This present conflict now moving toward a frightful and soul-testing climax has long been foreseen and prepared for. Humans actually cannot live and survive without reliance upon the God Spirit, as the hollowness of victory and defeat will eventually demonstrate.

But animal forces must needs be let run wild to prove to millions who cannot and will not learn any other way, that killing and destruction never brings happiness or security. Such a fact should be self-evident but it never *is* for *any* generation since each new physical body, undirected by spirit, responds only to the law of the jungle—kill or be killed! To "kill humans off" by self-seeking economic competition is simply a "more civilized form" of murder.

February 14, 1942

Things *will* work out for next week, in a manner quite satisfying to you after this long trying period of waiting.

Conditions are so upset these days and so constantly changing that it is exceedingly difficult to attain a settled state in anything.

For the world at large this situation is bound to grow steadily worse for a time, but you will be constructively active during the turbulent months to come—with attention being attracted more and more favorably toward you and your works.

Your faith and your efforts *will* be rewarded. Fear not and trust in these powers that have been revealed to you.

Turn now to your Bible for a confirming message of spiritual reassurance.

Opened on inspiration to the exact page and led to read Galatians 6: 4-11:

4 But let every man prove his own work, and then shall he have rejoicing in himself alone, and not in another.

5 For every man shall bear his own burden.

6 Let him that is taught in the word communicate unto him that teacheth in all good things.

7 Be not deceived; God is not mocked: for whatsoever a man soweth that shall he also reap.

8 For he that soweth to his flesh shall of the flesh reap corruption; but he that soweth to the Spirit shall of the Spirit reap life everlasting.

9 And let us not be weary in well doing for in due season we shall reap, if we faint not.

10 As we therefor have opportunity, let us do good unto all men, especially unto them who are of the household of faith.

11 Ye see how large a letter I have written unto you with mine own hand.

8

Further Communications

1942 - 1952

Diary *Chicago*
October 1, 1942

We devoted the entire a.m., Harold having developed an idea for a new book under the title *The Great Adventure of Your Soul*, to rereading the messages received from Ara while in California. As Harold started reading them, an inner voice directed, "Read as of now." We did so and were greatly moved and held spellbound by the predictions contained and the application of contents to our present situation. The messages seemed to substantiate the impression Harold had last night with respect to new developments in the offing. Marginal note: During his reading of the Ara messages, a title for another book came to Harold's mind, *Little Talks with Your Soul*. Harold felt that this could be inspirational in nature and partake of some of these rewritten messages.

Ara *Chicago*
November 12, 1942

Listen now in the night seasons, for a voice is soon to speak to you. This Voice can only be heard in the stillness of your inner temple wherein I, Ara, reside, to watch over the child that is your evolving soul.

"Except ye be as little children, ye cannot enter the Kingdom of Heaven," Christ Michael said, when on earth.

A child looks up to his human father without question and with all faith. You must become conscious of the child of your own spirit which your life experience is creating within you and have faith in me, who am acting for the Father as we work together to conceive a soul and give it embodiment for our joyous journey through the worlds of time and space, to come at last to the Home which the Father of all has provided for us.

The Father is mindful of your prayer, "Thy will be done." And yet, with you, as with many, the flesh is weak. "Of myself I am nothing," the sages of ages have said. And they have drawn from the night seasons, through close communion with those on high, the wisdom and sustenance so needful to great earth accomplishment.

Surrounding you and your dear one are a battery of powerful intelligences awaiting the earthly hour when you are to be called to the true work of the Kingdom.

Be not too disturbed during this trying waiting period. The planetary turmoil is upsetting to all human life and will be more so. But guidance and protection will be accorded you in moments of real and pressing need.

Meanwhile, give increasing spiritual ear to the instruction that is to come, and know that all is really well and the opportunity you seek will come.

Relax and feel my presence for I am truly with you. I am working in closest cooperation with him who indwells Martha for your destiny is as one and you will move forward together.

Addendum

Following the reception of the previous thoughts, while Harold was relaxing on the sofa and Martha was going over the notes taken on Tabamantia's visit to this planet[1], she came across

---

[1] Apocryphal Urantia messages which were shared with the Shermans.

mention of John the Potter. This awakened in Harold the recollection of an earlier impression which had come in a short time before but which he had let slip away into his subconscious.

"It is I, John, who have come to be with you during the work ahead, to help you keep burning the torch handed you by Abner."

Martha wrote this down and after a little Harold continued:

"The fire from this torch comes from God, the Father, and is the eternal-urge-heavenward ablaze in the heart of man. It is this fire which eventually consumes all things of the flesh and releases the evolving soul of man from the ashes of his otherwise binding earth experience. You have asked for the true meaning of fire. *Physical fire* destroys all temporal forms; *spiritual fire* transmutes. Without it there can be no illumination. As you progress you will yearn to be more and more consumed in it, for only in this manner can your higher self be forged."

As if in verification Harold was then impulsed to get the Bible and the dictionary. Opening the Bible first, his eyes fell immediately upon 2nd Kings 2-11.

"And it came to pass, as the still went on, and talked, that behold, there appeared a chariot of fire, and parted them both asunder; and Elijah went up by a whirlwind into heaven."

In the dictionary he found: ". . . to change by the action of fire, as in the making of *pottery*. Also that the synonym for *spirit* is *fire*.

While writing down the above thoughts for Harold it occurred to Martha that in the future, when Harold had unusual dreams which should be recorded, that she should get up and transcribe them as he spoke so that he would not be so likely to take himself out of the inspirational mood by the physical effort of writing. However, she said nothing as she was tired and did not want to even think of the possibility of having to get up, once in bed!

Later, as he was getting into bed, Harold suggested the very same idea; that he had thought perhaps the hours of taking notes on the Forum situation had developed in us an ability to work together smoothly in this manner. So we agreed to follow the dictation method in the future. We had no idea we would be called upon to try it so soon!

We were dropping off to sleep when Harold suddenly said, "Quick!, write this down!" And the following lines were given, the first two rapidly and the rest more slowly. The title was added the next morning.

SONS OF GOD

Hands he had not;
    Nor mouth, nor head, nor heart.
For in his world
    No form we know became himself a part.
And yet, a man he was—
    Another son of God—
    Who lived and died as you...
(A planet known as Od)
    The form is not the man;
The man is not the form,
    And worlds no end with creatures swarm
The wheel of life to run,
    As led they are by light within
Cast by Eternal Son.

Ara   *Chicago*
November 18, 1942

And fire it was that destroyed Cleodotus as he rushed in to save the records of the burning church in Philadelphia.

Rampant were the non-believers of this day bent on plundering and killing. In this church were the treasures of the believers—a rich store of wealthy goods to serve those who sought to keep alive the truth. There, also, was the prized wine flask which Cleodotus had raised to the tortured lips of Christ Michael—prized at the thought that it had touched the flesh of Him who had died at the hands of his own created beings.

This, and the priceless recorded words of the crucified Creator Son, Cleodotus vainly sought to rescue and preserve. He died pressing the bottle to his own lips, feeling close to Him whom he had succored on the day of His trial and betrayal.

Thus did Cleodotus, in league with Abner, pledge the new and final service which was to carry them down to this present day to stand guard again that no second betrayal of the true revelation of God, the Universal Father, should come to pass.

How seemingly alone has been the journey of those two and yet, few there are on earth today whose footsteps have been more lovingly guarded and guided.

Is it not fitting that they, who stood fast in that far distant day against the host of those who would have bartered the truths of Christ to personal gain in the market place, should now stand fast again to prevent the return of this great and truth destroying evil? Far greater is this present crime, for the truth was never more hungrily yearned for by mankind!

Urantia trembles in the balance of a mighty cataclysm or a mighty spiritual renaissance. The worlds of Nebadon look on in prayerful awe and anguished hope. They stand powerless against the rule of human will in the lives of men. This will must, of its own free choice, give way to the will of the Father or the ultimate certain destiny of the planet Urantia will be advanced into the centuries of time.

Stand firm, Cleodotus! You are not alone! She who is with you has been with you before. You have been tested in service and have not been found wanting. Much is soon to be revealed. Be of good cheer.

Ponder on the "ar" contained in the names Harold, Martha, Mary, Marcia and the name I give you.

The Seven[2]   *Chicago*
                                                        January 8, 1943

Hitler intends to launch a savage gas attack upon England in the spring. He also intends to use gas in an attempt to stop the advancing horde of Russians who will threaten to overrun Europe. He will tell the German people that they must annihilate or be annihilated. He has a chemical bomb invention which burns the oxygen out of the air over a sizeable area, causing death to all life in the vicinity.

This attack, if it comes, will be sudden and horrific, and mark the new and most terrible, as well as final stages of the war. Unhappily, unless England and America are prepared to retaliate in kind immediately and with great force and effectiveness, this last mad venture of Hitler may come close to succeeding.

The terrorizing nature of the assault will have such a terrific impact upon the consciousness of those who have loved ones in the fighting forces on the fronts affected by Hitler's gas barrage that they will set up a frenzied clamor, amounting to nationwide panic, for the war to be stopped. Thus with a world sickened and nauseated almost beyond endurance, Hitler will entertain one last desperate hope that he can turn back the fate which is closing in upon him.

He has reserved a fleet of heavy bombers especially equipped for chemical warfare to release in this last assault. The suddenness of such an intended attack will be its most potent weapon. Allied leaders will not believe that any adversary would dare loose such inhuman tools of warfare.

---

[2] Harry Loose taught the Shermans that spiritual work was done in groups of seven, that each person should "find" his own seven. This communication was apparently dictated by a group who signed off with "We Are Seven."

Hitler believes he can subjugate England in from two to three weeks through such an attack. More important even than destroying munition plants is the necessity for bombing all chemical factories and warehouses where these bombs are stored.

1943 will outrank all others in bloodshed, in this or previous times, but the very stepped-up intensity of the conflict will speed its devastating end. The world will be left gasping, nerve-exhausted and shattered at its finish.

We see these potentialities clearly and these conditions forming in what is future time to you. Nothing exceeds this information in importance at the present moment. Hitler knows that his attempt to bomb England and Russia out of the war has failed. He knows that the only other possible weapon left to him is gas. He will attempt to justify its use when he feels the time has arrived, even describing it as an humanitarian measure for bringing a speedy end to the war and restoring peace to the world.

This is a fact which must be faced by the Allied War Council and methods devised to checkmate in advance of its possible happening. It is regrettable, in your present state of so called civilized nations among you which abhor the fiendish use of gas and are pledged not to employ it unless it is used against you, shall be the ones to suffer most for that very reason.

Gas warfare is quick; it is paralyzing. He who gets in the first blows has a tremendous advantage. Could Hitler reach America, in your present woeful state of unpreparedness against gas, the loss of human life would be unimaginable. England herself is none too well equipped, even with gas masks, for the type of gas which may be used.

While driving Hitler back on many fronts, with the growing assurance of ultimate victory which will result, the imminent danger of this surprise gas attack must not be lost sight of. If this can be circumvented, Hitler can be defeated yet this year. If not, the United States and Russia will be left to carry a tremendous burden, since Hitler will use the threat of gas to keep subjugated all the peoples of the conquered countries who otherwise would revolt. He will point to England as the horrible example of what he will visit upon Holland, Denmark, Belgium, Rumania, France, Norway and all other countries unless they accede to his demands.

You can out-produce Hitler but you cannot outdo him in fiendishness. This to your credit but also to your peril.

The gas warfare campaign has already been mapped out and the most vital points marked for attack where the leaders of allied war forces are known or thought to be located. The attempt will be to rob by death most of the allied leadership in these first attacks. If it were possible to make a token raid on Washington for the effect on world morale, this would be done. Hitler knows America is too vast, even if he had the equipment, to accomplish much against her in the time left to him.

It may be necessary for America, should this turn in the war take place, to resort to gas and to mercilessly move in upon Japan to eliminate this threat as quickly as possible in order to meet the far more serious threat which Germany will become under such conditions.

German High Command is even now nervously checking reverses on different war fronts and arguing as to the time schedule for such a designed attack. England and America must guard against a dangerous complacency and Germany may purposely let it be thought that she is near defeat.

The solution of this situation must rest with those on Earth. Some allied leaders know well this possibility but too many of them dismiss it as beyond even Hitler's inhumanity to introduce. In this belief they err. We know whereof we speak.

This communication is to remain unsigned for our identities would mean nothing to those who might consider the information and warning contained herein. A way may be opened for a presentation of this document to those who should properly know about it. You are to follow what impulses come to you.

Let us only say, in thanking you for receiving this transmission, that We Are Seven.

The Seven   *Chicago*
February 6, 1943

Coming toward you in time is a matchless opportunity to reach the consciousness of mankind.

You, who have held yourself free throughout life of any and all affiliation with church, organization or society, are now free to present Truth and Inspiration acceptable to millions of human creatures who are *not* free.

What you will be inspired to say to them will give them a freedom of mind and heart and spirit they have never experienced before on this earth.

You will gladden the souls of a hungry multitude who are seeking God and cannot find Him in the established places of worship nor even within their own selves.

The force of what you will say is destined to awaken in countless minds an awareness of The Presence.

You are to be a "door opener" for the fragment of God to enter consciously into the lives of all who have ears to hear. These fragments will then begin their mighty task of organizing their human instruments into a spiritual band which will serve as a stabilizing influence in every community reached by your voice.

What you will say will bring about the most potent resistance to evil forces that has yet been set up as a means of combating the last fiendish efforts of designing factions to subjugate, through fear and hate and threat of economic poverty, the masses of the people.

There are now, prepared and waiting to join forces with you, humans in high places and low who will appear on the scene in increasing numbers at the command of your voice.

Those whom you serve will gladly serve you, for the god of commerce will smile upon them while the real God, your Father, accomplishes His purposes in the ways of men.

Witness that your destined life work is commencing as the war prepares to enter its most violent and frightening stages.

Witness that the beginning days of chaos and travail, such as mankind has never known, are approaching.

Witness that the awesome vision you beheld as a boy, who early put aside childish things, is now, soon, to become a part of the reality of the world.

Witness a gathering of the clan of humans who are to serve with you through the great trials that are to come.

Sufficient unto each day, up to this present moment, has been your knowledge thereof, and this is said of Martha as it is said of yourself, for she, too, came to serve with you in this same great mission for which you have both so nobly qualified in the trial by fire, the trial by faith as is required of all to whom is to be entrusted the spiritual destiny of millions of now lost and bewildered human creatures.

To you both much has been given and yet, never at any time until it was earned. Your way has been lonely but you have never been left in darkness. Always have there been spiritual lights along the path, even when you failed to perceive them, but now more instruction will soon need to be given for the tempo of your life expression is destined to quicken as there crystallizes about you, both in earth and heavenly form, a spirit force of great power and designed purpose.

You will be no less responsible for your own conduct, physically, mentally and spiritually, but through maintaining your present attitude you will be increasingly more receptive to guidance.

Millions of humans will come to rely upon the attitude of mind and spirit which you maintain in your radio talks[3] and your personal contacts. As you live and express, so in a great measure will they strive to live and express for, in a modern way, you are again setting forth a spiritual pattern of living and laying the foundation for wide public reception of the Book of Urantia.

The field must be plowed before the seed can be planted—a field which is just now stagnant with dead and decaying worldly things and which can only be fertilized to fruitfulness by the sunlight of Truth.

The road ahead is not easy but you have not been led to your present appointed task by easy stages.

No steel is tempered without heat. No human soul is forged except through the fire of life's trials. Whom God loveth, He chasteneth.

Proceed fearlessly.

You are about to take the torch completely into your own right hand and keep it lifted high above your head that its light may shine out and bring new life and new hope to your fellow creatures struggling, blindly and fearsomely on this dark planet.

Be of good cheer. You will not be alone in this mighty task and remember, they who are seven on earth are ever supported by "we who are seven" here.

We share with you now the peace of the Father as we bid you "goodnight" but not farewell.

Dream   *Chicago*
February 13, 1943

Early this A.M. in a dream state, Harold found himself seated in a garden facing a kindly, impressive, long bearded man

---
[3] Harold's radio show, Your Key to Happiness, was about to launch in Chicago.

with locks of reddish brown and a loose robe. He was speaking slowly, earnestly and in deep musical tones.

After the first few sentences Harold was awakened but the words still rang in his consciousness and he got up and wrote them down. He felt the thoughts, as expressed by this man, continuing, so he rapidly wrote them down for so long as they kept coming to consciousness,

The exact words as apparently spoken by this being were:

"Majestic as the sprays of two dogs playing in the sun, one peeing south, the other north.

"I tell you I have seen nothing more beautiful than the universes revealed in the rainbow hues contained in these cast-off sprays, or in the interplay of forces disported by the firefly—a matchless projection of God's forces, too simple for mere man to comprehend.

"Fire—the *fire* in the dogs' urine caught by the sun's rays; *fire* in the throbbing glow of a firefly's wormlike body; *fire* in the chance sharp meeting of two stones; *fire* in the rough passions of two wild beasts and *fire* in the quick tempers of two creatures who call themselves humans. Fire, untamed, uncontrolled, through and around and in all forms of life.

"*Fire*, my son! Think on it! Think on it!

"I stroke this beard and a universe of forces crackles in it—the *fire* of electricity!

"*Fire, fire, fire!*

"Seek God not in unusual, remote places. Find Him where He is, in all things.

"*Fire* in the fever of a sick child, in the heat of a mother's breast, and *fire*, unknown to you, in the cold wastes of space.

"Think on it! Think on it!

"*Fire* of imagination which leaps at inspiration's bidding.

"Flames, both cold and hot, but still *fire*. What is it?

"Solve the mystery of *fire* and you approach the mystery of being.

"Think, my son! And let there be a conflagration in your own soul to burn out all that is unworthy.

"*Fire!* Without it no universes are born; no universes of affection exists between man or animal or God; no light shines in distant stars and no reflected image strikes the eye. Without it, no forms could be or, once having been, ever change.

"*Fire*, my son, is the essence of all that is God's word expressing in the unfathomable and eternally expanding realms of time and space.

"Think on it—for to know *fire* is to know yourself!"

• • •

After returning to bed, the following thought came:

"You are a part of God's great adventure in the worlds of time and space."

The Seven Prophecy   *Chicago*
August 2, 1943

A great light will appear in the heavens, as it seems now, in the year 1945.

Its brilliance will startle all mankind.

It will cast an illumination over the entire earth.

It will mark the beginning of the great change to take place on this planet.

It will awaken all humans to the realization that there is a power far greater than themselves.

Scientists looking through earth's telescopes will describe this light as a far-distant universe being destroyed, the light rays of which have just reached us in this present day.

The presence of this great phenomenon in the heavens will cause the greatest religious revival known to man.

All grades of intelligence will be caused to think now, not in global terms, but in cosmic terms.

This great light will deal the forces of darkness the greatest blow since the appearance of Christ on this earth.

When it comes it will be the signal to those enfleshed on missions of service that the time for the Truth is at hand.

Awestruck millions will search their souls as never before.

There will arrive at this time a host of higher beings assigned to work with the new spiritual leaders who will take their places among their fellow humans.

The floodgates of revelation will be opened up in science and man will commence to grope from threatened chaos toward a new harmony of being with all things.

The time is not foreordained; it is to be synchronous with developments on your planet.

The first evidence of this great light will be detected in the East when it comes.

It will be a forerunner of Christ Michael's promised return to the World of the Cross.

But *when* He shall return is known alone to the Father.

When you will have left this earth it will be with the knowledge that mankind is, at last, on the upward path and this could not be truly said of any previous age in which you have served.

We who are Seven have spoken.

Free Will   ***Chicago***
September 27, 1943

Man's exercise of free will increases in direct proportion to his understanding of God's purpose in his life.

Man *is* limited by the physical—environment and circumstances—but he still possesses a power within him capable of rising above all external influences.

Man's will *is* free, else he would be a mechanistic creature reacting the same in each instance to every experience which comes to him. But no two men react the same to any similar experience. Each in free to react as he feels and thinks at the moment.

To deny that man has free will is to deny that he has any part of God in him, for God's will is not limited; and when man learns to follow God's will, all things in line with his life's purpose are made possible to him. This is true of the lowest as well as the highest mortals.

The will of some men is more free than others for they are more enlightened, but this does not mean that others may not enlarge their capacity or exercise of this free will.

No will is free that follows blindly the dictates of the flesh.

This is not even will—it is animal desire.

If man did not possess free will, God's promise of an ever-widening higher life would be hollow mockery, for how can man attain anything beyond this material world in which he finds himself if he has not the power to choose and aspire?

Simply to decide that one wishes to live after death is not a manifestation of will. Such a decision may be motivated entirely by fear and not by a spiritual urge to take an upward path. Man's Thought Adjuster is not fooled. He reads the record of Man's life and sees written thereon the soulful imprint of his life's freewill decisions. This is man's passport to the training worlds of time and space.

There are few human creatures, even today, who have humbled themselves enough to say—and to really mean it when the prayer is uttered—"Thy will be done."

Herein is contained the fullest expression of free will. For the great majority, their wills are joined with God's only in moments of great crises and human need. It is in these moments that humans come to know they are more than animal.

Were humans not free they could never reach out and join their lives with God. But each human, however low, can call upon the Father and receive an answer. It is not true that God only unites His life with lowly creature man when man decides that he wishes to start the Paradise ascent. A place has been provided for every human creature before even birth takes place and he is given free will to choose that place. Would he even have the consciousness or the urge to aspire to such a place if his will were limited?

As a matter of individual fact, each human's will becomes more free as he grows in life experience—more wisdom of choice is given, more courage to choose and more faith to support the choice.

Of course, free will is relative but so is every activity on earth and in heaven as it relates to God, the Supreme.

Freedom of choice exists throughout the universe. It is the invisible stairway upon which all beings, high or low, climb to God.

The Seven Prophecy   *Chicago*
October 17, 1943

Something of a tragic nature is forming as a potential happening within the next two to three months which is apt to rob the U.S. and England of some of their foremost diplomats.

The Germans are determined, if possible, to waylay them on their trips to and from Russia and to destroy the special planes carrying them as they did the plane carrying Leslie Howard and other officials of a secondary nature.

This time it is felt that a destroying of these personalities en route to Russia would quite probably upset the timing and planning of the final gigantic allied assault upon Germany and Japan.

No effort will be spared to determine the route to be taken by the planes bearing these noted persons.

Actually, their loss would eventually bring about a closer, more sympathetic and understanding bond between England,

Russia and the U.S. But, should this happen, the effect would be temporarily world startling.

However, new leaders and new men of vision have been prepared, knowingly and unknowingly, to meet just such an emergency who will bring to the world situation a different plan of action, much more free from old-line procedures and techniques.

It is eternally true: You cannot get new wine from old bottles. For this reason many catastrophic events are actually proven, as measured by time and subsequent developments, to have been blessings in disguise.

Too many humans, the way your world is now organized, outserve their usefulness and yet remain in power. This condition, in time of emergency, can constitute the number-one peril to a nation.

Since free will cannot be preempted, oft-times those prepared and ready to successfully take over are compelled to stand by until the propitious moment for service has passed. The torch then passes out of their willing hands into the grasp of other men and women coming along in other moments of time.

Secretary Hull[4] is not a well man and he is a greatly worried and disturbed soul tonight. He feels not only his earth years but the pressing weight of his responsibilities, for he realizes that failure of this three-ply conference can release forces which can well bring about the end of the Democratic Party's reign in America.

Actually, the type of union and relationship between these three powerful governments is eventually not going to be at all along the lines now indicated.

---

[4] Referring to then Secretary of State Cordell Hull (1871-1955). In 1945 Hull received the Nobel Peace Prize for his role in establishing the United Nations.

The possibility of a strong reactionary move on Germany's part is daily growing more imminent. She may ultimately lose the war but, just now, and for the past few months, has been largely consolidating her position on all her fronts at considerable loss to her attackers. The Germans reason that he who attacks pays a much dearer price than he who strategically retreats over soil of his enemies.

The Germans still feel that the worst they can get from this war is a stalemate which they will consider a victory.

Should the war last a year or two longer, the economic factors of colossal waste and expense will loom so large as to take precedence over every other reason for continuing this slaughter and destruction.

The events of the next three months should determine whether this war may come to a sudden and unexpected early conclusion or whether it will be prolonged.

Watch carefully and read between the lines. You will see much to confirm what has been herein said.

We, who are Seven, have once more spoken.

Thoughts *Chicago*
August 1944

Upon the shores of all the yesterdays of time all that I am today was born.

Speak well, then, of the Dead.

For, resurrected now within myself is every bloody struggle to attain which has brought to man this consciousness of God in which the hope of life eternal long has lain.

And so, upon the canvas of each soul, we paint anew vague recollected pictures of the past and add our touch of color to the scene and leave it just a little more progressed for those who follow to complete the rest.

The canvas then, is bigger than ourselves.

We find, at last, it fills the universe.

We paint with brushes dipped in blood of life, a blood that's mixed with world of strife.

And seldom do we see whereof we paint, our vision is so clouded here on earth.

But one day we will see the canvas whole when we have forged, within ourselves, a soul.

Thoughts *Chicago*
September 18, 1945

If you could see your Soul, resident in your flesh body, it would appear to you as a tapering, candle-like, blue flame burning in consciousness. Its light casts an electrochemical glow over the intricate, ever functioning, delicate mechanism of the brain. It is reactionary to every thought and deed of the operating intelligence.

Since the Soul is the substance of the Eternal in man, it is building for eternity by consuming in the fire of its own radiance all that which has no survival value. The Soul has been truly called "the divine spark in man." It is a transmuter of all that is worthwhile on the human level to that higher and ever-expanding dimension of spirituality.

It is the duty of the Thought Adjuster to sift the thoughts of the entity and pass them through the mystic fire of the Soul. All that is of value for the progressive evolution of the entity beyond this life is transmuted to a higher form while that which is only of temporal worth is consumed.

The entity arrives in the state beyond death with a memory record of good and bad as well as consequent yearnings. But the body form of this life-giving Soul substance no longer permits the exercise of evil desires in a physical way. For this reason some degraded entities seek a return to earth and possession of the bodies of weak-willed mortals still enfleshed that they may find renewed physical outlet for their continuing evil nature. However, the great majority of those who pass on and who carry over much that is evil seek to have it consumed in the fire of their Soul's ever-increasing radiation as they will to progress.

The Soul is a creative fire which is fanned by the spiritual deeds of man. The finer the deeds, the more brightly it burns. We cannot, as yet, stand the radiance of our own God-given Soul which is the dimmest reflection of God's own radiance. In the eternity to come, as we through our deeds evolve our Souls, their radiance will become indescribably transcendent when the vast assemblage of these Souls will provide a spectacle of power and light utterly beyond finite comprehension.

When fusion takes place the perfected intelligence of the Thought Adjuster is blended with the self of the entity by the experientially developed fire of the Soul raised to such a spiritual degree that union with God the Father then becomes instantly and eternally possible.

This union gives to the new self a directional power over the Soul substance so that participation in experiences beyond time and space, unknown and unknowable till then, becomes existent.

Experience is the never-ending fuel of Soul fire.

Experience, itself, is a substance. We can touch it thru memory. We can feel it mentally. We can remake and reshape it for more refined and more mature uses and we can retain always its essence in the form of Soul growth.

Thoughts   *Chicago*
September 1946

This I have learned—that true religion is never found in churches but only in the heart of Man.

All churches are but the symbol of Man's organized attempt to find God. As such, they should be respected but not revered, for stone cathedrals never saved a human soul.

When Man passes by a church because it is not of his faith, this alone condemns all churches for there is but one God, and Man should not divide himself in worship of Him. If each man's faith in one and the same God led to all churches, then would God dwell in them through the united devotion of His children.

But, since a Mohammedan cannot find God outside his own faith, nor a Buddhist, nor a follower of Confucius, nor a Hindu, nor a, Jew, nor a Christian, nor any other worshipper of a sect or a cult or an ism, then this very separativeness is damning the Brotherhood of Man and denying the Fatherhood of God.

For how can God rule in the hearts of men when men rule that God exists for them only in and through their own faiths and would war against their fellow creatures to enforce or impose this rule?

Faith in God is a product of Man's inner experience and can never be bestowed by church affiliation.

Through war, many churches have been destroyed. They are being rebuilt, stone by stone, but nothing is being built into the heart and soul of man.

God stands in the pulpit of each heart and speaks an everlasting sermon to all who seek him there.

He says, "You can find Me in the heart of every fellow human in need for he is searching for Me as are you and, in doing for him what you can, whether his skin is black or white or yellow, in the common brotherhood that is born of this friendly human service, both have entered My Presence. A faith in each other has led to a faith in Me. Could such a spiritual adventure befall each earthly creature, the stone walls of churchly prejudice would be rent asunder by the true manifestation of My Spirit in the heart of Man.

Thoughts *Arkansas*
November 29, 1952

The Thinker is not the thing thought or the thing that thinks, nor any aggregation of things already thought but is, instead, the sensitized receiver of sensory impressions of all things outside its Center of Being which gives to the Thinker an awareness of individual existence surrounded by everything else that is.

The Thinker's reaction to these sensory impressions creates thought, and how the Thinker reacts to the things thought determines the Thinker's selection of life experiences and growth of consciousness.

Thought is, therefore, the process by which the Soul of the Thinker is developed. But thought is not the Soul because the Soul can have an I AM awareness beyond thought; and thought, as commonly interpreted, implies words and language, whereas true communication, understanding and knowledge take place through feeling.

The real Thinker is he who senses reality by direct contact with it, on the highest, most innermost plane of his being, beyond the reach of thought processes where dwells the eternal awareness which says, "Be still and know that I am God."

9
Poems
1942-43

ETERNAL GLORY

They die beyond our world of sense
    But live in fuller measure.
Our senses limit what we know
    And, blind to spirit treasure,
We struggle here encased in flesh—
    Our souls the body may enmesh,
The animal in us is rife
    From origin of bestial strife.
But, as we climb our Godward way,
    We loose our hold on house of clay
And death is given as the key
    To realms which, now, we cannot see,
But which were destined from the first
    To quench man's growing spirit thirst.
Tho' low our being in His sight,
    Our climb from darkness into light
Will one day find us by His side—
    Earth sons in whom He has great pride.
Mere chapter of a greater story
    That leads us to eternal glory!

—November 20, 1942

WHEN GOD SPEAKS

The end for which beginning was
    Is coming unto man.
He now must face what sinning does
    As best the human can.
His free will choice of sense desires
    Has warped his growing soul
And cut him off from spirit fires
    Which light man's inner goal.
Long ages past man's stumbling feet
    Have bruised his sensual way.
Life's pages are a balance sheet
    Demanding that man pay.
No longer can the human wait
    His passions to appease;
The tempo of his spirit fate
    Will bring him to his knees
And cause the God in him to speak,
    As crushed he is and low,
Reduced, at last, in spirit meek,
    The truth he now must know.
For man the animal must leave—
    This time the way divides—
The human part, itself, may grieve.
    The soul, with spirit guides,
Will rise to heights before undreamed,
    As mankind sees the way,
And naught will be as it has seemed
    When God's Word rules the day.

—November 22, 1942

OUR SPIRIT VOICE

If strive you would to seek the good
    That's buried deep within you,
You'll need to reach the spirit guide
    Beyond your nerve and sinew.
The animal in which you live
    Is powerless to aid you
And you must sense the greater truth,
    It's really God who made you!
A kingdom lives within your mind
    In which your spirit dwells
But you, in blindness, fast are tied
    And live a thousand hells.
A voice within you fain would speak
    To point unerring way,
But you, with ears of spirit dulled,
    Hear not what God may say.
When soul, from body reaches up
    To realms where it belongs
And catches, now and then, the tone
    Of truthful spirit songs.
For harmony abounds on high
    And with man must reside
Before the animal in him
    Will yield and step aside.
Your spirit voice determines choice
    Of steps you yet must take
And he who listens guides his feet
    His destiny to make.

—November 22, 1942

A UNIVERSE IS BORN

About a billion years ago,
    Before this world was made,
God's architects surveyed this space
    In which their plans were laid.
They martialed all the lines of force
    And energies that flowed
From out the central universe
    Of God's supreme abode.
And all was motion in this sphere,
    Dark islands swirling round,
As force directors gave commands
    That matter might abound
In all the myriad forms designed
    For evolution here,
Before the breath of life from God
    Was destined to appear.
Long eons passed and vast the task
    Of beings from on high
As step by step this mighty work
    Brought light to this dark sky.
A sun blazed forth, its brilliant rays
    Seen gleaming from afar
By creatures watching breathlessly
    Upon a distant star.
And joy there was in all the realms
    Of life-pervaded space
When birth of this new universe
    By God's decree took place.
The neighboring suns, in greeting joined
    Their warm and friendly hands
To grip this new sun's fiery form
    In strong, magnetic bands.

And hold, in gravity embrace,
    These planets newly born
Which Sons of God, in earthly form
    Would one day soon adorn.
Oh wondrous is the pattern schemed
    For lowly creature man
Which his evolving soul must weave,
    Each strand as best it can!
Oh merciful is God on high,
    In love and wisdom just,
As he awaits man's climb to Him
    Through human faith and trust!
Oh glorious is the goal ahead—
    Unspeakably sublime—
When man's evolving soul survives
    The worlds of space and time!

—November 24, 1942

SONS OF GOD

Before all time and space God was;
    His presence, Paradise,
A stationary central Isle
    Unbounded, without size.
Dimension, yes, in consciousness,
    Beyond our grasping here,
Abiding place of Father-Son
    A timeless, spaceless sphere.
But Son in Father could not be,
    And time and space were born
That God might take eternity
    His being to be shorn
Of countless other Sons of Him—
    Descendants of this One—
On whom God smiled and found no fault,
    His own Eternal Son.
So greatly pleased was God in Him,
    His very first creation,
He spoke the word that freed this Son
    To share God's great elation
In moving out from Paradise,
    With tools of time and space,
To fashion worlds of finite power
    And found the human race.
A creature man, quite animal,
    In early stature made,
With Son of God a Creator Son
    To keep him unafraid—
A Father watching over him—
    The selfsame loving care
That God, through His Eternal Son
    With all alike does share

As universes new spring forth,
    In stately grand procession;
With always for the beings there
    A spirit intercession
That God, through all ascending Sons,
    His own may glorify
As they evolve through time and space
    To mansion worlds on high.
Eternal Son is our birthright—
    Sonship with God above—
Our goal beyond all time and space
    Sustained alone by Love.

—November 25, 1942

THE VOICE WITHIN

Though time and space their fetters place
    Upon the mind of man,
Through Faith, each soul may reach beyond
    And sense God's mighty plan.
No story can be told complete
    To struggling humans here
For many cannot face the Truth
    While lives are ruled by Fear.
And many more are quite content
    To go their stumbling way
Indifferent to the Voice within
    And what it tries to say.
"Oh Man, the road ahead is long
    And far away your goal.
Look up, not down, give spirit wings
    And free your earthbound Soul!"
Each step you take can be toward God
    With vision rightly centered.
You may walk with Him and talk with Him
    The moment He has entered
Your sacred realms of mind and heart
    Upon your invitation.
And great will be the changes wrought;
    It's true of *all* creation
For soon as man the door unlocks,
    And lets the God force in,
He starts to climb upon a path
    That leads away from sin.
The flesh itself is always weak
    So destined from the first
For man was not intended here
    To quench his spirit thirst.

But, even so, the plan of God
    Man's free will choice allowed
That he might climb to worldly heights
    Of which he might be proud.
Thus far, man's willful, lustful sway
    Has pushed God quite aside
And in the depths of untold souls
    Their faith has all but died.
To gain again the vision lost
    Through hateful, Godless living,
A cataclysmic time must come,
    And man must be forgiving
Of all the evil done to him
    As he has done to others;
And come to know and love *all* men
    As equals and as brothers
For God indwells the lowest soul
    As He indwells the highest.
To those who seek to do His will
    His presence comes the nighest.
And Faith in Him, unfalteringly,
    Throughout all grief and strife
Will lead your soul unerringly
    Into Eternal Life.

—November 27, 1942

THROUGH DEATH

The fear of death has panicked Man
    From time he came to earth—
And yet, through death, the soul of him
    Is given its free birth.
Imprisoned deep in fleshly house,
    The Godward side of man
Has sought to leave the animal
    Since human state began.
For spirit joined with flesh that day,
    When freewill choice took place,
And God, from that great moment on,
    Indwelt this lowly race.
His architects, who planned this world
    And all its forms of life,
Had witnessed through the years untold
    Its upward, struggling strife.
That Man, of all the creatures here,
    Should have evolved so high,
Brought joy to hosts administering
    As God, Himself, drew nigh.
For all creation seeks to find
    From what source it has sprung
Since all life-forms are but the beads
    Upon which life is strung.
But freewill choice may be attained
    By every worldly creature.
This faculty, when once achieved,
    Becomes its spirit teacher,
Preparing it for realms beyond,
    Through trial and error here.
The choice of good or bad by man,
    His vision none too clear,

Keeps lifting him, slow step by step,
    Upon the rungs of time
And builds for him a soul within
    Which starts its homeward climb.
For God, Creator of all things,
    In Heaven-world resides
And draws all seeking souls to Him;
    Unerringly he guides.
For man to die, is then to gain
    A blessed sweet release
From all that plagued him here on earth
    And kept his soul from peace.
The animal, in which he lived,
    Returns its form to dust
But, rising out of it is man,
    In God's Love placing trust.
And standing by his quivering soul,
    As death his body takes,
A part of God, in spirit form,
    The bonds of soul now breaks.
A seraphim, an angel shape,
    Appears on mission graced
And into her safe custody
    Man's sleeping soul is placed.
A transport waits with passengers
    Bound for the mansion worlds
With heavenly insignia
    Upon its side unfurled.
Majestic is the trip through space
    Unconscious though the soul!
Conditioned is man's spirit now
    For waking at its goal.
God's messenger who dwelt with him
    Has made report on High—

A record of the earthly life
    And of man's soulful try
To rise above the animal,
    Its fear and lust and hate,
And claim his promised destiny
    Before it was too late.
But now God speaks and what He says
    Sends spirit guide a-winging
"This is my Son in whom I'm pleased,"
    All angel voices singing.
And then the soul of man bestirs,
    Sweet music fills his ears
And, in the twinkling of an eye,
    His new-born form appears.
God's spirit guide is by his side
    To take him by the hand
And lead him onward on his path
    With all the joyous band
Of those who have survived this life
    Upon the World of Cross,
And know, at last, that in God's Love
    There never can be loss.

—December 2, 1942

THIS WORLD OF CROSS

Three days Christ Michael lay in death,
    The same as creature man.
He rose in spirit just to prove
    That what He did we can.
The path He trod we are to tread;
    No darkness can enshroud
His Spirit is a light to us
    A guide through storm and cloud
As fleshly mists rise up, at last,
    And earthly shadows fall,
While man's soul struggles to be free
    And leave the worldly pall
Of low vibrating forces here
    (a part of this dark planet)
Which strive to bind the soul of man
    And finally to ban it
From going on to realms beyond,
    As God, Himself decreed
Before this earth, through Lucifer,
    Its evil ways did breed.
O struggling man, you lost the path
    In ages now far gone!
Your free will choice was led astray
    By leaders who did wrong.
And fellow creatures, in that day,
    Who followed those they trusted
Became the servants, not of God,
    Their souls with sin encrusted,
Until conditions here on earth
    The Angel Beings sickened.
And man, in anguish, cried for help
    That spirit might be quickened

Else he might lose all he had gained
    On stumbling, upward path;
Nor find escape from Satan's sway
    And God's eternal wrath,
The destiny of man was set
    From day he made first choice
To build for self a better world
    And listen to God's voice.
But, through default of those on High,
    Assigned to guide man's way,
Strange things were brought to pass on earth
    A long and evil day,
Which only a Creator Son,
    Whose children were in danger,
Could save by being born on earth.
    And so, it was a manger
That first embraced this Son of God—
    In last bestowal life—
Who chose to visit this dark world
    With sin and lust most rife.
A world where Adam, yes, and Eve,
    Had also failed in mission
By fusing with the races here
    And weakening through emission,
Life's plasmic forces given them
    For raising high the stock
That man might gain new spirit power
    And set ahead the clock
Of his evolving earthly state,
    So much in need of aid,
With man beset, within, without,
    His very soul afraid.
How sorrowfully Creator Son
    Looked down on what He saw!

And He knew then that only He
    Could now restore God's law.
To do this, He must needs come down
    From His accustomed place
To be then born as other men,
    A human form to grace.
A baby born as other babes,
    And yet, as not another
E'en though of actual flesh and blood
    And earthly father mother;
A babe into a growing man
    With angel hosts attending,
Creator Son on earth as man,
    And not the least pretending
But living just as man has lived
    And evermore must live,
Nor calling on His higher powers
    Surcease from trials to give;
Experiencing the ills of flesh
    And, tempted as we are,
By evil loosed upon this earth
    Which God will not yet bar
Since, in His mercy infinite,
    All creatures gone astray
Are given every soulful chance
    To find again their way.
Christ Michael then, in coming here,
    Existing as a creature,
Sought by living as He did
    To be man's spirit teacher;
To show to man the truths of God,
    The universe on high,
The kingdom of another world
    To which man's soul could fly

Escaping from the house of flesh
    So battered, weak and weary
And leaving, far behind, this earth
    With pain and grief so dreary.
But man, in anguished ignorance,
    The Master could not see
Nor recognize in human form
    Just who He chanced to be;
That He who walked this earth in flesh
    Was really his Creator,
A drama ne'er before so great
    In any world theater.
And O! the tragic climax when,
    A cross with nails was plied
To fasten bleeding hands and feet
    A lance wound in His side,
The broken form of this, our King,
    Beloved Son of God,
Was crucified by us that day
    And beat with stone and rod
And spat upon and deep reviled
    By children of His own
Whom He had come to earth to save.
    And they, His Truth disowned!
And yet, in giving up His life
    As man, himself, must give it,
He bore the cross that we must bear.
    We're not to die, but live it!
For how we live and what we think,
    If choose we do God's will
Is all that really counts on earth
    And gives our soul its fill
Unto the day when comes the call
    And we through death must pass,

With spirit freed, our soul now joins
    A graduating class
Of beings destined to partake
    Of joys prepared on high;
Reward for all we've suffered here
    From One who, too, did die
That we again might live with Him
    In worlds of finer hue
And know the love He holds for us
    Eternally is true.

—December 5, 1942

UNTIL THE DAY

Your sun was in the heavens
    Near the outer rim of space
A hundred million years ago
    When birth of earth took place.
A blazing, hissing meteor
    Came hurtling through the sky
And passed so close to whirling sun,
    It brought destruction nigh.
For one great moment all the fate
    Of what was yet to be
Hung in that tortured atmosphere
    As struggling sun tore free!
But there was left a gaping hole
    As from its side was rent
A molten mass, exploding still
    With energy unspent
Urantia—the baby's name,
    Its fathers name unknown,
As mother sun was left to care
    For new born earth alone
While out of sight, in realms beyond,
    This fiery comet sped
Creating other mother suns
    Across whose path it fled.
The baby earth remained within
    Her mother-sun's fond grasp
And spun about in bounds of space
    Her breath a flaming gasp
Of white hot gases—cooling now
    And swiftly taking form,
A rounded shape in circuit swung
    To join celestial swarm

Of planets by the billions
    Which mother suns attend,
A universe unfolding
    In a scheme that has no end.
And when the earth, Urantia,
    Through time reached solid state
Great mountains rose and moisture came
    To help the heat abate.
'Twas then, from realms on high to earth,
    Life Carriers were sent
With special seeds of life to plant,
    By God's divine consent,
Which architects in Heaven world
    Had lovingly designed
To try in evolution here
    Each type to be refined
And, through this great experiment,
    Find form to house a soul
Since God decrees that time and space
    Has creature man as goal,
Though in what shape on different worlds
    This consciousness may rise
Not even those who bring life's seeds
    Can accurately surmise,
Once that creation starts on earth
    In friendly ocean deep.
The first life forms in salt brine grow
    Before on land they creep
Then vertebra in animal
    Begins to take its place
And, jelly like, the brain is born
    Experience sets the pace.
Now from all fours the creature rears
    And reaches toward the sky

As thick in skull it stares about
    And dully wonders why
It moves and has its being so
    Among such fiendish beasts
That it must daily kill to live
    As on all life it feasts.
God's mystery here is unrevealed
    And free will unattained
As lower forms of life evolve
    The animal unchained.
And angel hosts watch anxiously
    The creatures here below
Which, still beneath the human state,
    Through trial and suffering grow
Until a blend of type occurs
    Each seeking something higher.
On earth, the change through lemur came
    And spirit first took fire
When one fine male a female sought
    And led her far away
That they might make a loving home
    Above the bestial sway
And look for some force from beyond
    To guide their stumbling feet,
Faint sensing that they held within
    A power that would defeat
The terrors of the storm and quake,
    The perils of the wild,
And let them rear in safety there
    A newborn type of child.
Oh! then it was that God looked down
    And sent a part of Him

To dwell within each groping mind,
    E'en though perception dim,
That as the race of man evolved,
    Which these two now would start,
A growing consciousness of God
    Would fill each seeking heart.
Andon and Fonta were their names
    The first two earthly creatures
Who lifted man within God's sight
    And brought him spirit teachers—
Those marvelous Beings from on high
    Who dwell within us all
And evermore, have led since then,
    Responding to each call
That struggling man has made on them,
    Their guidance ever sure.
For these God fragments seek in man
    A soul that will endure
Beyond the change that man calls death
    When God's plan is revealed
Another world as real as this
    With ever widening field
For man to rise from animal
    And leave this state behind
Until the day in spirit form,
    He comes to know God's mind.
Though long ago this earth they walked
    First creatures to aspire
Andon and Fonta still await
    To greet those tried by fire
Of all the evils loosed on earth
    O'er which their souls have won

And they will not seek higher state
    Until this day is done
'Til struggling man has put an end
    To all his mortal strife
And this dark earth is bathed, at last,
    In God's own Light and Life.

—January 18, 1943

ETERNAL SPRING

Oh! sing me a song of hope and cheer
    And the gladsome news that God is here
Oh! sing me a song that can lift my heart
    And to my spirit now impart
The courage to do what I know is right
    As day by day in this mortal fight
I face the evils [problems] as best I can
    Of struggling, striving, creature man.
Oh! give me a song that I may sing,
    The notes of the joyous birds in spring,
Which herald to all, "New life is here!
    New life is born this time of year!"
Oh! let me view God's plan anew
    And thus preserve all that is true
Amidst this world of shame and sin
    That my soul must be nurtured in
God give me roots deep down in Thee
    That I may stand firm as a tree
Against the gales of flesh desires
    Which keep from man what he aspires.
Oh! let me ever mindful be
    That song of life has come from Thee.
If false notes creep into this song
    Remind me I have done Thee wrong.
Be with my soul oh! Lord, I pray.
    The night is long and short the day
For darkness tries to close me round
    With greed and lust my feet are bound.
But long as I may hear Thy voice,
    And long as granted me the choice
Of seeking with my soul the light,
    I know, oh! God, I'll feel Thy might.

>   And with Thy strength a part of me,
>   I'll lead my soul to victory
>   O'er all the evil rampant here;
>   O'er all the hate, deceit and fear
>   Until the day I draw last breath
>   And give this body up to death
>   And soul stands free—a bird on wing
>   To sing now of Eternal Spring!
>
>   —*January 22, 1943*

EQUALITY

All men are not as equals born
    Nor was it so at first;
God did not make one creature blessed
    And leave another cursed.
An ape that chatters in a tree
    With skull so cramped and small
Was never cousin to the man
    Who deep in sin did fall.
The fish that swim beneath the sea,,
    The slimy snakes that creep,
Are all evolving in their way
    And to their forms they keep.
Nothing is lost that lives and breathes
    All has a place within God's plan
From lowest of the low on earth
    To highest of the high in man.
The ant is happy at his work,
    The bee hums round the flowers,
The vulture waits on meat's decay,
    All life some life devours.
For man is yet an animal
    Related is his past
To forms long since become extinct
    As earthly die was cast.
Once launched upon the stream of time,
    Man's destiny was sure.
The act of free choice brought to him
    A soul that could endure.
It mattered not what flesh he wore,
    How addled then the brain,
For now man had a part of God
    In him to help attain,

Man sees so dimly, here below,
    God's great and mighty scheme;
He frets about his place in life,
    The often shattered dream,
The knowledge that his fellow man
    Outranks in wealth and power
The hopeless quest of happiness
    That hounds him by the hour,
The desperate strife to do the right
    In world of flesh gone mad,
The cry to God for faith to save
    The little that he had.
No—men as equals do not live
    In fleshly life on earth
But in each striving where he is
    Man proves his own soul's worth.
For man is not to end his days
    When his form goes to dust.
He's risen from a low estate
    And, in God placing trust,
Will leave the animal behind
    Which dominated here
While newborn soul escapes through death
    And leaves this worldly sphere.
The busy ants, the bees that hum,
    The vultures stalking prey.
We cannot see a place for them
    Beyond earth's little day.
And yet, in ways we know not of,
    All life in God exists
And myriad forms are being lost
    Within eternal mists.
Our puny minds cannot divine
    The reason for it all.

But should we doubt the care of Him
    Who notes a sparrow's fall?
Creator of this universe
    With countless worlds in space?
Unthinkable that God for man
    Has not reserved a place!
That He would let us go astray
    By higher ones misled!
To not withdraw man's freewill gift,
    But send His Son, instead,
Is pledge to man that God has heard
    His lowly human cry
And gives each soul equality
    When man's turn comes to die.

                            —*January 23, 1943*

BLEST IS THE MAN

An aimless futile life this is,
    If God has no part in it,
And all who try to live without
    Are learning by the minute
That they possess no power alone
    With which to meet life's trials,
For man, himself, is animal
    And filled with worldly wiles.
'Tis only when he reaches up
    To grasp God's strong right hand.
That man is more than animal
    And takes his spirit stand.
But he who thinks there is no God
    And seeks his own free will
Comes soon or late to realize
    That life is less than nil.
No joy is there in riches gained,
    No pride in victories won,
No happiness in self sought goals
    When God less race is run.
Blest is the man who wakes in time
    And hears the voice within
A voice that guides and lifts him up
    Above this world of sin;
An entity—a part of God—
    That dwells within his mind
On whom he now may call at will
    And truth forever find;
A Presence lighting bright his way
    Each day a radiant dawn
As God in man now leads him on
    And bids all sin be gone.

A purpose fills man's heart and soul;
    Each triumph brings real joy.
He knows, at last, why struggle here
    With pain is an alloy.
He knows that through the trials of flesh
    With many earth desires,
A soul is being forged by man
    In crucible of fires
In which the deeds of man are stirred
    If good he need not fear it
The ashes of this life are left;
    Surviving is his spirit.
New form it takes, of chemicals
    Not known upon this earth,
And soul of man is clothed by God
    In raiment of rare worth,
While spirit Guide, who tried by fire
    This soul while yet in flesh,
Now fuses with the spirit form
    The two in one enmesh.
And this does God co join with man,
    While man his own self keeps
And evermore unfolds with God
    As joys untold he reaps!

—January 23, 1943

THROUGH FAITH ALONE

No animal on earth but man
    Can reach, through faith, to God.
All other life, in lower state,
    Is ruled by instinct's rod.
The sense bar man's progress still,
    As he his pathway seeks
Away from carnal, earthly things
    With which his body reeks.
A something deep in man now stirs—
    No part of his long past—
A something other life has not
    Which came to man at last,
When he, a creature, gained free will
    And raised himself above
The myriad forms of other life
    To seek, a-now, God's love.
For He, of whom we're all a part,
    Has granted to us here
A spirit guide to dwell within
    Who holds our soul most dear.
To us, as humans, came this light
    Direct from God on high,
And once it lodged within our souls
    We knew that God was nigh.
No creature reaching man's estate,
    On other worlds in space,
Is left to seek his God alone
    Without this saving grace.
The senses cannot testify
    That God in man resides
And that the voice within is He
    Who with our soul abides.

'Tis only when man stills each sense
    That he to God's height rises
And leaves behind all in this world
    Which soul of him despises.
Through faith alone man calls to God
    And God within him answers.
The flesh of man would bind him round,
    Destroy the soul like cancers
Which fibrous grow, and spread like sin,
    Throughout each body part—
And without aid from Spirit Guide
    Man's soul would soon lose heart.
The forces ill upon this earth
    Would sweep him fast away
And leave him naught but animal
    As he was once—that day
He first emerged from sea of life
    And crawled upon all fours
And free will choice had not been born
    To open Heaven's doors,
When man looked up, and self aware,
    Asked who and what he was,
A something happened in him then
    As man thinks, now, he does
And man's first thought the pattern set
    Which all men since have followed.
Each thought and act in mind is checked
    If good, the Spirit hallowed;
If bad, man loses touch with God
    And lives in flesh alone
Until with pain and anguish rent,
    All sin he would disown.
Once more, through faith, he reaches up
    To clasp God by the hand

And strives through his evolving soul
    His love to understand;
A love which reaches down to man
    From God's supreme abode
And helps him, step by step, along
    Life's hard and bloody road.
No thought or act is faith itself
    But rather a condition,
A state of consciousness for man,
    Which lifts him from perdition,
Uniting him through Spirit Guide,
    With power of God untold,
And filling his weak vessel mind
    With all that it can hold
Of truth and wisdom and of love
    O'er spirit circuit sent
No limit placed on this great store
    Except by man's dissent.
So long as by his faith in God,
    He keeps this circuit closed
His Spirit Guide will bring to him
    A life that is composed
Of all the elements he needs
    To build aright his soul
Until, at last, through God, he knows
    That death is not his goal.

—February 11, 1943

www.ingramcontent.com/pod-product-compliance
Lightning Source LLC
Chambersburg PA
CBHW031443040426
42444CB00007B/949